THE WORSHIP OF THE CHURCH

THE CHURCH'S TEACHING

I   THE HOLY SCRIPTURES

II   CHAPTERS IN CHURCH HISTORY

III   THE FAITH OF THE CHURCH

IV   THE WORSHIP OF THE CHURCH

In Preparation

CHRISTIAN LIVING

THE EPISCOPAL CHURCH AT WORK

VOLUME FOUR

The Worship
of the Church

MASSEY H. SHEPHERD, Jr.

*With the assistance of the Authors' Committee of the
Department of Christian Education of
The Protestant Episcopal Church*

GREENWICH · CONNECTICUT · 1952

Foreword

The Worship of the Church is the fourth book to be published in THE CHURCH'S TEACHING series. While Dr. Shepherd has written the entire text of this book, the Authors' Committee and the Department of Christian Education are greatly indebted to Dr. Brown-Serman and the Rev. C. Kilmer Myers for extensive preliminary work.

We have tried to avoid writing a history of liturgies, as interesting and as useful as such a book would be. Instead we have labored to give the Church a volume which would deliver to the reader as quickly and as accurately as possible the particular genius of the worship life of the Book of Common Prayer.

The Prayer Book is not just a book of prayers nor even a treasury of services of worship of our Church. It is a way of life. It is the particular way of life in which Episcopalians participate in the drama of redemption. Since this drama has been the central theme of the preceding books, *The Holy Scriptures, Chapters in Church History,* and *The Faith of the Church,* the reader will find familiar ground from which he can explore with fresh understanding our corporate means of spiritual strength.

JOHN HEUSS
VESPER O. WARD

· *v*

Preface

The scope of this book is defined both by its title and by its place in the series, THE CHURCH'S TEACHING. It concerns itself solely with the interpretation of the public, corporate worship of the Church, and in particular with that branch of Christ's Church whose heritage of worship is enshrined in the American Book of Common Prayer. Though the book may be studied independently of other volumes in the series, it does presuppose the critical, historical, and doctrinal positions of the three volumes that have preceded it—*The Holy Scriptures, Chapters in Church History,* and *The Faith of the Church.*

Though there is an intimate relation between the private devotional practices of individual Christians and their public, corporate worship, there is no discussion in this volume of the problems and disciplines of private prayer and meditation. This subject will undoubtedly be treated in the forthcoming volume, *Christian Living.* Nor does this volume treat of the philosophy and psychology of religious worship in general. We are rather concerned with a particular form of worship that is rooted in the Christian Faith and is embodied concretely in the liturgy of the Episcopal Church. Limitations of space make it impossible even to explore the interesting parallels of the rites of the American Prayer Book with those in other provinces of the

Anglican Communion, much less in other branches of Christ's Holy Catholic Church. One will find in the bibliography a number of titles of books that deal adequately with these comparisons and relationships.

The gratitude of the author can never be adequately expressed for the encouragement, criticism, and, above all, the Christian fellowship of his colleagues on the Authors' Committee.

MASSEY H. SHEPHERD, JR.

Contents

PART I

The Principles of
Christian Worship

CHAPTER ONE

The Motives for Corporate Worship

"THESE PERSONS, being Christians, have held an assembly for the Eucharist, contrary to the edict of the Emperors Diocletian and Maximian." So read the charge made by the magistrates of the town of Abitina in North Africa, before the court of the Roman proconsul in Carthage, on the twelfth day of February, A.D. 304.

"What is your rank?" inquired the proconsul Anulinus of the first prisoner presented to him.

"I am a senator," replied Dativus.

"Were you present in the assembly?"

"I am a Christian and I was present in the assembly."

Straightway the proconsul ordered him to be suspended on the rack and his body torn by the barbed hooks. . . .

Then Saturninus, the priest, was arraigned for combat.

The proconsul asked, "Did you, contrary to the orders of the emperors, arrange for these persons to hold an assembly?"

Saturninus replied, "Certainly. We celebrated the Eucharist."

"Why?"

"Because the Eucharist cannot be abandoned."

As soon as he said this, the proconsul ordered him to be put immediately on the rack with Dativus. . . .

Then Felix, a son of Saturninus and a reader in the Church, came forward to the contest. Whereupon the proconsul inquired of him, "I am not asking you if you are a Christian. You can hold your peace about that! But were you one of the assembly; and do you possess any copies of the Scriptures?"

"As if a Christian could exist without the Eucharist, or the Eucharist be celebrated without a Christian!" answered Felix. "Don't you know that a Christian is constituted by the Eucharist, and the Eucharist by a Christian? Neither avails without the other. We celebrated our assembly right gloriously. We always convene at the Eucharist for the reading of the Lord's Scriptures."

Enraged by the confession, Anulinus ordered Felix to be beaten with clubs. . . .

Last of all, the lad Hilarion, son of Saturninus, remained to be tried. The proconsul said to him, "Will you follow your father and your brothers?"

"I am a Christian," he confessed in his youthful voice. "Of my own free will I joined the assembly with my father and my brothers."

The proconsul then tried to terrify the boy by threatening torments— (he was so unaware that he was fighting not against men, but against God in his holy martyrs)— and said, "I shall cut off your hair and your nose and your ears, and then let you go."

To this Hilarion replied clearly, "Do what you please. I am a Christian."

The proconsul ordered him to be returned to prison.

And all heard Hilarion's voice crying with great joy, "Thanks be to God." [1]

Such, in part, is the actual record of the confession made by a congregation of forty-nine Christians who had met together in the home of their priest to fulfill "their bounden duty and service." Their story is by no means singular. From the days of the apostles until Constantine's famous edict of toleration in 313, Christian disciples lived in constant danger of losing life and property if apprehended by the police or turned over to the magistrates by informing neighbors and acquaintances. Accounted traitors to society and the commonweal, they were denied by law the right to assemble with one another for common acts of devotion to their Lord. No matter how quietly, how discreetly they gathered for worship in their homes, or in the cemeteries where they laid their dead, Christians were never free from the threat of molestation and violence. [2]

"Day by day we are besieged; day by day we are betrayed," complained Tertullian; "oftentimes in the very midst of our meetings and gatherings, we are surprised by an assault." [3] Yet whatever the peril and risk, these Christians refused to absent themselves from their association of common worship and allegiance. They had found in it that "treasure hid in a field," that "pearl of great price,"

---

[1] These paragraphs are translated from the Latin Acts of St. Saturninus and companions. The original text may be found in Migne, *Patrologia Latina*, VIII, 688 ff. Excerpts in English are given in B. J. Kidd, *Documents Illustrative of the History of the Church*, Vol. I (to A.D. 313), London: S.P.C.K., 1920, No. 172, pp. 221-24.

[2] For the story of the early persecutions, see *Chapters in Church History*, pp. 14-22.

[3] Tertullian, *Apology* 7.

for which a man will sell all that he has in order to possess it. In the company of prayer they were certain to lay hold upon their Lord in the glory and the strength of His abiding presence; for He had promised "where two or three are gathered together in my name, there am I in the midst of them" (Matt. 18:20). In the mysterious actions of offering, blessing and sharing one loaf and one cup, in remembrance of Him, they consummated a real communion with His risen and exalted life, and had a foretaste of "the powers of the world to come."

What brought them together was no desire of satisfying merely inward, personal longings for fellowship with God. This they could and did find in the secret chambers of their private devotions. Nor was it simply a response to that inner urge in men for social companionship with people of like sentiments and interests. The compelling urgency towards corporate worship arose out of the very nature of Christian faith itself. The grace of the new covenant established by God's redeeming work in Christ was imparted to men not as isolated individuals, but as "very members incorporate in the mystical body" of Christ Himself. Throughout the New Testament and early Christian literature this organic conception of the Church as one body of many interdependent members runs like a golden thread.[4] And it was precisely in the sphere of corporate worship that this organic relationship of Christians one with another realized its most telling expression. It is no wonder that the Roman authorities of state believed, and rightly so, that if they could prevent Christians from assem-

---

[4] See *The Holy Scriptures*, pp. 160-66, and *The Faith of the Church*, pp. 128 ff.

bling together they could destroy Christianity root and branch.

In our modern Western culture, with its prevailing philosophy of individualism, there is a widespread notion, even shared by many professing Christians, that a man who absents himself from the corporate worship of the Church harms no one but himself. Such a conception is just the reverse of the early Christians' approach to worship. Separation from the fellowship meant separation from the Body of Christ. Without each one's participation, that Body was dismembered of a necessary limb, and to that extent its unity was broken and its vital force impaired. In a comment upon our Lord's saying, "he that gathereth not with me scattereth abroad," an early Church manual of worship and discipline put the matter this way: "Since you are the members of Christ, do not scatter yourselves from the Church by not assembling. For since you have Christ for your head, as He promised, do not be neglectful of yourselves nor deprive the Saviour of His members, nor rend and scatter His Body." [5]

Especially in the Eucharist was the oneness of fellowship in Christ exhibited in all its fullness. It was not a rite performed by the clergy on behalf of such individual Christians as felt disposed to make the effort to attend. It was the common action of all the redeemed children of God, in obedience to Christ's command, to offer and present themselves, souls and bodies, as a living sacrifice united with and conformed to their Lord's uttermost oblation of Himself on Calvary. Only thus could they, the Church, realize

---

[5] From the *Didascalia apostolorum* xiii, edited by R. H. Connolly, New York: Oxford University Press, 1929, p. 125.

in supreme degree that which they were called and sanctified to be by their baptism into Christ—namely, members one of another in Him. Lest the unity of this offering be impaired in the slightest measure, it was their custom to take the sacramental gifts regularly to every member unable to attend the common gathering—the sick and those in prison for their profession of the Name of Christ. And this was done, too, with the additional risk of detection by the police and further attacks of persecution. For such dutiful devotion one with another the martyrs "loved not their lives unto the death."

INDIVIDUALISM AND INDIFFERENCE

It is difficult for us American Christians today to recapture in our imagination the resolute and valorous spirit that carried the early Christians to their corporate worship. Going to church does not involve us in any hazard to our reputations, much less to our lives. As no law compels us to go to church, so no law hinders us from doing so. Among the blessings of liberty guaranteed to us by the supreme law of our land, none is more highly cherished than the first article of our Bill of Rights: "Congress shall make no law respecting an establishment of religion, or prohibiting the free exercise thereof." Moreover the law assists us in many ways in the practice of our liberty of conscience. Sunday is a legal holiday. So is Christmas, and in some places Good Friday. Church services are protected from any interference by disturbers of the peace. Church properties are tax exempt. We are guaranteed complete freedom to propagandize and teach our religious convictions and practices to any persons interested in them.

Religious toleration seems to us so fundamentally reasonable and just that we are prone to forget that it is neither immemorially old nor universally admitted. Many sincere people have believed that tolerance in religion assumes an indifference to truth. And truth is not a thing indifferent. Though intolerance need not lead to coercive measures, religious persecution, whether by civil power or ecclesiastical authority, has in fact filled many pages in the annals of history. Nor is the record of it as yet filled up and completed. The more devoted men are to their convictions, religious or irreligious as the case may be, the more difficult it is for them to be tolerant and forbearing: especially if they have at hand forces capable of imposing their beliefs and practices upon others. Yet again and again history has shown the practical futility of wars of religion and of repressive measures against religious nonconformists.[6] Force cannot compel belief, nor can penalties stamp it out. "God himself," said Thomas Jefferson, "will not save men against their wills."

Christian faith at its purest and best is a passionate conviction that admits of no compromise with other faiths. Deeply impressed upon our conscience are our Lord's appeal to and example of obedience to the first commandment of God's law: "Thou shalt worship the Lord thy God, and him only shalt thou serve" (Matt. 4:10). This law not only contains our sole religious allegiance; it transcends, if need be, even the highest loyalties of our earthly existence, those of family and country. Our Lord Jesus Christ promised His disciples that they would be persecuted for such a faith; indeed, that they would find foes in their own families and households. "He that loveth father or mother more than me is not worthy of me: and

---

[6] See *Chapters in Church History*, pp. 183-90.

he that loveth son or daughter more than me is not worthy of me" (Matt. 10:37). It should not surprise us, therefore, that a demand of such absolute loyalty has induced many Christians who have suffered harsh oppression to turn the tables on their persecutors when they have had the opportunity. Yet never in the New Testament is there any suggestion that the Christian faith should be propagated by any other means than preaching and teaching and the testimony of exemplary character.

In our modern era the growth of toleration in religion has come in the wake of new philosophies secular in spirit and individualistic in emphasis. This circumstance has had the unfortunate effect of suggesting to many minds that one religion is as good or as bad as another, and that religious belief and practice are purely matters of private opinion. The impact of this outlook in modern thought has resulted in the steady divorce of religion from other social concerns of life, whether they be politics, economics, science or culture. The famous dictum of Camille Cavour, "a free church in a free state," has come to mean the complete freedom of church and state from any interest in or concern for each other.[7] The commonest heresy of our times—one not always encountered only in the Church—is the claim that religion deals *only* with spiritual things, or with the life beyond death, or with saving individual souls. But it is precisely because Christ redeems men's bodies as well as their souls, and saves them through incorporation into the holy society of His Body, that Christianity must have an interest in all the material and the social concerns of human life.

---

[7] See *Christian Living*, Volume V in THE CHURCH'S TEACHING series, for a discussion of the problem of Church-State relations.

The gravest danger inherent in the exaggerations of religious individualism is that such a point of view disarms us of the most potent and effective weapon against the materialistic, totalitarian systems that have arisen in our time. The new persecutors of our age would have no quarrel with Christianity if it confined itself solely to other-world interests of purely private opinions. Hitler's "Director of Philosophic Outlook," Dr. Alfred Rosenberg, reminded the Churches that they "have fundamentally but one task, that of making known to those men upon whom they have a claim the Church's belief in the Beyond. The earth on which they live is no longer in the least the affair of the Church." [8] Such men cannot endure Christ's claim to the whole of human existence, and the Church's insistence that all relationships of life be set in the light and under the judgments of its faith and worship. There exists in our own day a great company of martyrs and confessors. They are the men and women who resolutely refuse to allow their witness to Christ to be isolated from the rest of life by a secular-minded individualism on the one hand, or by a materialistic collectivism on the other. The former destroys our social responsibility one to another; the latter degrades our individual worth and dignity as the children of God.

The principle of religious freedom is so deep-rooted in our American tradition that, short of losing our national independence, we are not likely to face the menace of outward restraints upon the free exercise of worship according to our convictions. It is this very liberty of choice we enjoy that compels us to examine the motives behind our

---

[8] Quoted in G. Vlastos, *Christian Faith and Democracy*, New York: Association Press, 1938, p. 44.

Christian practice. For it is well to remind ourselves that the total number of professing Christians in the United States today does not add up to half of the population. If we subtract from this total those who are only casual or occasional attendants at public worship, we have a remainder of faithful adherents who are nothing more than a tolerated minority. Going to church on a Sunday morning is neither the conventional thing to do, as we sometimes imagine, nor is it necessarily a mark of respectability. No doubt some people do attend public worship as a social convention or as a mark of respectability, if not out of sheer habit. But the generation of Mr. Day, immortalized in *Life With Father,* is a thing of the past. Mr. Day accepted churches "as unquestionably as he did banks. They were substantial old structures, they were respectable, decent, and venerable . . . frequented by the right sort of people." For these reasons he insisted upon his family's attendance at church. "The right thing to do for religion was to go to some good church on Sundays."

Of course, many persons who make no regular practice of participating in the Church's worship will stoutly defend its continuance by others from a vague sense of its good to society. They will admit that worship is morally beneficial to those who find it interesting or congenial, and that, as such, it makes them better citizens. The value they place upon worship is by way of its practical results in conduct. Such a judgment is by no means confined to those outside the Christian fellowship; it is one of the commonest pleas whereby church-goers justify their own devotion. Worship makes them feel better, behave better, live better. There is nothing inherently wrong in this attitude. As a tree is judged by its fruits, so a man's faith is tested by his works, and his worship by its effects. We all know full well the disrepute into which our religion falls when we fail to live up to the tenets of our prayers. Certainly there would be more conversions to our fellowship of common prayer if more of us who now profess it would show forth the praise of God "not only with our lips, but in our lives."

The values placed upon public worship by our individualistic society are by no means limited to the support that worship gives to public and social morality. Frequently those who participate in worship justify their practice by purely self-centered interests. People respond to worship, positively or negatively as the case may be, according to the personal satisfactions that it affords. Our likes and dislikes become the controlling motives that lead us to choose this service or that. It may be the preacher, the music, the ritual and ceremony; or it may be the kind of people who frequent this church or that, their friendliness or aloofness, their sophistication or lack of it. Again and again we meet people whose primary canon of judgment upon any particular act of corporate worship is the self-regarding consideration of what they themselves get out of it. It does not occur to them to think first of what they might contribute to it out of selfless devotion or useful talents.

A common example of this self-centered attitude is the person who remarks of his casual attendance at church that he can worship God just as well at home, or in the park, or out in the country, as he can in a pew with fellow Christians. What such a person usually means to say is that worship does not interest him because it does not provide him with what he believes he really wants. There are other people who desire the benefit of religious rites only when they are in trouble or in some specific personal need. When life is running smoothly they have no concern for the fellowship of prayer, no desire to give thanks to God for all his manifold blessings upon them. But the deadliest perversion of self-centered worship is to be found among those who would use the Church's services for worldly advantage. The occasional rites, such as Baptism, Holy Matrimony, and Burial of the Dead, are special victims of this kind of covetousness. But there are many other varieties of it—the politician who is seen in church only when he is electioneering; the business man who calculates how much his prominence in church will help his trade; the social climber who desires to cover ambition with the aura of the Church's respectability. The curious thing is that such persons do not see how transparently vulgar their attitude is. "Thou shalt not be as the hypocrites are," said our Lord, "for they love to pray . . . that they may be seen of men" (Matt. 6:5).

THE MOTIVE OF NEED

It would be most unjust to condemn outright all self-regarding motivations that lead people to common worship. Most of us who attend church on Sunday morning, if we are honest with ourselves, will confess that we do so, in part at least, because we feel the need of it for our own individual selves. Many Christians who were not trained in childhood in the habit and the duty of worship have found their first conscious response to corporate worship arising from a sense of personal need. The satisfactions of these needs sought in worship vary, of course, from individual to individual. For some they are primarily social, for others intellectual or psychological; for others still they are more distinctly religious in character.

1. *Social need.* Certainly one of the basic motives of need is the desire for friendship and companionship. Man is by nature a social animal. He becomes a recluse only out of sheer necessity or by a deliberate and willful cultivation of "the solitary's lot." The welcome sign on a church door has brought many a lonely individual out of a city crowd, and many a new family settled in a strange community into their first real experience of the fellowship of prayer and service.

"All sorts and conditions of men" can and do find in the Church's worship bonds that transcend both the natural and the artificial divisions of humankind, whether they be of race, nationality, wealth, education or social status. Granted all the smugness and snobbery that vitiates the sense of brotherhood in the worship of many congregations, it still remains true that many individuals have found outstretched to them most readily and unconditionally in the company of common prayer a loving acceptance and appreciation. Time and again it does happen—

> In Christ there is no East or West,
> In him no South or North,
> But one great fellowship of love
> Thro'out the whole wide earth.

Unless worship does satisfy the hunger of men for gracious company it cannot properly claim allegiance to Him who shall judge it by the precept: "I was a stranger, and ye took me in."

2. *Intellectual need.* Another motive of need stems from the perplexities and confusions of life. In our own

times this kind of insecurity is very prevalent. People are looking for guidance, for certainties, for an anchorage in fixed and abiding principles that give meaning and perspective as well as final goals to their lives—it may be with respect to intimate personal problems or to the disorders and dilemmas of our common society as a whole. They want an answer to the prayer that "among the sundry and manifold changes of the world, our hearts may surely there be fixed, where true joys are to be found" (Prayer Book, p. 174). Call it what you will—revelation, illuminaton, insight—that is the inquiry they make of Christian worship. And they will "shop around" from church to church in quest of it, whether from the preacher or the liturgy or possibly from both.

3. *Psychological need.* Sometimes, it is true, what is really wanted is a safe refuge from the struggle with life's perplexities, a cover behind secure affirmations of faith, the reassurance of long-used, familiar patterns of prayer. Wavering convictions are steadied and weakened loyalties are encouraged by what a distinguished philosopher has called the force of social confirmation. "When the voice of the past as heard in the ritual becomes the voice of our living fellows too, when one hears other worshippers on all sides repeating in tones of conviction the doctrines which one has always thought one believed, the force of social confirmation becomes, at least for the moment, too great to be resisted, and faith marches triumphant over doubt." [9]

Others again will be drawn to worship for the moments it affords of uplifting and steadying peace, for the thoughts and remembrances that—in Wordsworth's lines—

---

[9] J. B. Pratt, *The Religious Consciousness, A Psychological Study,* New York: Macmillan, 1926, pp. 282-83.

> Uphold us, cherish, and have power to make
> Our noisy years seem moments in the being
> Of the eternal Silence.

Surely there is a place in worship for the refreshing calm of recollection and contemplation, away from what Henry Scott Holland called "the city's crowded clangor." But worship is justly reproached when it retreats into an atmosphere of sentimentality or unreality, overmuch detached from the sterner issues of life. We must be ever on our guard lest the ancient splendor of the Church's ritual, clothed in the art forms and ceremonial of past generations, be turned not to the uplifting and enrichment of our lives but to an escape from them. The "comfortable words" of our Saviour Christ and the presence of His Holy Spirit, the Comforter, are indeed a solace to the fainthearted, the dispirited and the fearful. Yet we must remember that the root of the word "comfort" does not mean consolation, but encouragement, strength and cheer.

4. *Religious need.* In every congregation there are found those whose private devotions are insufficient to satisfy deep longings of the spirit. There is the sinner seeking assurance in the power and commandment given to Christ's ministers "to declare and pronounce to his people, being penitent, the Absolution and Remission of their sins" (Prayer Book, pp. 7, 24). There is the recipient of some special grace and blessing who, like the Psalmist, would pay his vows of gratitude unto the Lord "in the sight of all his people, in the courts of the Lord's house." There is the person bearing some pressing burden of petition and of intercession, who desires the supporting concern of the prayers of the congregation. Above all, there are those who hunger and thirst for some sensible touch of

the presence of God, to cleanse, restore and empower. Though not unmindful of His abiding and sustaining presence everywhere, they find Him without fail, as in no other place and in no other way, in that

> . . . gift that maketh whole;
> The bread that is Christ's Flesh, for food,
> The wine that is the Saviour's Blood.

THE MOTIVE OF DUTY

Not only a consciousness of personal need prompts us to worship with our fellow Christians; we are also drawn to church on Sundays from a sense of duty. In fact, the very recognition of the need arouses, in the conscience, the bidding to supply what is wanting. And just as our needs vary from individual to individual, so do our respective calls to duty—whether to ourselves or to society, to God or to His Church.

1. *Duty to self and society.* To some persons the duty of worship is primarily conceived as an obligation to themselves. They desire the full equipment of the whole man, well-rounded through the proper and dutiful nourishment of the soul no less than of the mind and body. Others view their duty to worship God in His Church from the vantage point of social responsibility. Parents feel that they owe the example of participation in worship to their children. Citizens support it for its contribution to the well-being of their community and country. Undergirding their sense of obligation is a conscientious loyalty to the principles for which the Church stands, the services it has rendered to themselves or to others, and the hope that it offers for a better world-society.

2. *Duty to God*. Christians also believe that worship is a duty owed to God. It is the way of acknowledging His lordship over life, of expressing gratitude for His provident goodness, of confessing our failures to obey His righteous will and of receiving His forgiveness.

> So when they cried unto the Lord in their trouble,
>   he delivered them out of their distress.
> He sent his word, and healed them;
>   and they were saved from their destruction.
> O that men would therefore praise the Lord for
>   his goodness; and declare the wonders that he
>   doeth for the children of men! (Psalm 107:19-21.)

In the accepted etiquette of society a man feels duty bound to show gratitude for favors extended to him, especially when they have been given to him freely and undeservedly. Nor is such a duty in the least burdensome. So a Christian finds his highest pleasure in the fulfillment of his duty to praise the Lord "and forget not all his benefits." At this level the motive of duty is transformed into a motive of love.

3. *Duty to the Church*. Also implicit in the motive of duty is an acceptance of obedience to the divine command and of loyalty to the discipline of the Church. The Offices of Instruction in the Prayer Book list among the "bounden duties" of a member of the Church the obligation "to worship God every Sunday in his Church" (p. 291). This statement is something more than a pious suggestion. It is the law of the Church. One of the canons of the Episcopal Church states specifically:

All persons within this Church shall celebrate and keep the Lord's Day, commonly called Sunday, by regular participation in the public worship of the Church, by hearing the Word of God read and taught, and by other acts of devotion and works of charity, using all godly and sober conversation.[10]

Ultimately this demand rests upon the divine law of the Fourth Commandment: "Remember that thou keep holy the Sabbath day." Our Lord did not annul this law, but He transformed the spirit of its observance. The Sabbath rest did not mean for Him, as it did for many of the Jews, merely a prohibition of physical labor and work. He stressed the positive opportunity that the Sabbath afforded for worship and for works of mercy and love.[11] Thus when the early Christians substituted the observance of Sunday in place of the Jewish Sabbath they made it the day pre-eminent for the celebration of the Eucharist and the agapes or love-feasts of charity for the poor.[12]

Now the Eucharistic celebration is itself an act of obedience to the command of Christ: "this do in remembrance of me." For this reason the Prayer Book describes the Eucharist in one place by the phrase "our bounden duty and service" (p. 81). And in the third Exhortation at the end of the Holy Communion it speaks of our "duty to receive the Communion in remembrance of the sacrifice of his death, as he himself hath commanded" (p. 89). The Church's law does not prescribe the frequency of the celebration and reception of Holy Communion, nor does it suggest that the Holy Communion is the only legitimate

[10] Canon 19. This canon, with slight verbal changes made in 1904, goes back to the primary General Convention of 1789.

[11] See Matt. 12:1-13 and parallels in Mark and Luke.

[12] For the origin and meaning of Sunday, see Chapter V and *The Holy Scriptures*, p. 164.

service of corporate worship on Sundays. What the Church does expect of its members is that they communicate in the Eucharist regularly, and that every Sunday be a holy day of obligation for the common worship of the faithful people of God. Surely no devout member of the Church attends its worship solely out of a sense of duty. But willful neglect of the fellowship of praise and prayer is and must be a burden to his conscience towards God and toward his brother in the household of faith.

THE MOTIVE OF LOVE

Both the need and the duty of worship, in the hearts of converted Christian people, are transformed and trans-figured by a fervent love of worship and joy in it. Regular exercise in corporate worship only serves to increase their appetite for it. They share the Psalmist's enthusiasm:

> I was glad when they said unto me,
> We will go into the house of the Lord. (122:1.)

In an age such as ours, when neither law nor social convention impels people to church, when Sunday affords innumerable, competing attractions of recreation and entertainment, it is fair to say that most people who attend public worship have in some measure a love of it over and above the appeals of other choices. The drawing power of worship may be the inspiration or the helpfulness of the parson's sermon, or the splendor of the liturgy with all its artistic accompaniments. It may be simply the friendliness of religious fellowship.

Where parochial life maintains among its members the atmosphere of a family, and the joys and sorrows of every member are shared in affectionate intimacy and concern, love of the brotherhood imparts a very special attraction to common worship. Even a dull sermon, a poor anthem, or an unimpressive edifice will not cast a pall upon the delight the members have in meeting one with another in this new relationship. The place of meeting itself enshrines hallowed memories and associations—of vows that have been promised, of trials and temptations borne and overcome, and of affections stirred to life. And there, too, in ways especially dear, is found the "mystic sweet communion with those whose rest is won."

Nor is that "kindly affection one to another with brotherly love" necessarily any the less in larger city congregations whose members are for the most part unacquainted. "Any one," wrote Bishop Brent, "who tries to be unselfish and to act in the common concerns of life with reference to his neighbour's interests, any one who has elsewhere learned ever so little about intercession, cannot be unmindful when he comes to church of those who worship by his side, strangers though they be. By the exercise of sympathy, sympathy which he has learned to kindle with less at hand to quicken it to life than that given by the living, breathing forms near by, he can bring close to him his fellow-worshippers, moving into the shadow of their intercessions as well as calling them in to share his own." [13] For the oneness of this fellowship has its point of meeting in Christ, who is the Head of the Body. And those whose joy is in the Head have love for all His members.

Indeed, the final Christian motive of all worship is love and joy in God—what the Psalms call delight in the Lord. In the ensuing chapter we shall see that this love is a

[13] Charles H. Brent, *With God in the World*, New York: Longmans, 1900, p. 92.

responsive act, a returning of the initiative of God's love toward us. It is, as we have already intimated, the outreach of gratitude for all "the wonders that he doeth for the children of men." It is summed up, with a conciseness unsurpassed, in a single sentence of the General Thanksgiving: "We bless thee for our creation, preservation, and all the blessings of this life; but above all"—and here one notes the distinctive Christian response of love—"for thine inestimable love in the redemption of the world by our Lord Jesus Christ; for the means of grace, and for the hope of glory" (Prayer Book, pp. 19, 33).

Our Lord Himself said, "And I, if I be lifted up from the earth, will draw all men unto me" (John 12:32). And this is true. For in His incarnate and redeeming life men see revealed both the height and depth of God's self-giving and man's obedient love. And there are countless hosts of men and women and children in every generation and in every coast and clime who go to worship in order to see Him lifted up in word and sacrament, and in the visible charity of His Body, the Church. The more clearly they see Him there, the more dearly they love Him there. And in that love their lives are conformed more and more to His image and likeness. Worship becomes, therefore, both the means and the end of attaining to our lives' fullest powers and possibilities—where we are "made one body with him, that he may dwell in us, and we in him."

CHAPTER TWO

The Elements of Corporate Worship

WHATEVER MOTIVES and desires draw us together for common worship, when we take our places in church we are soon conscious of a number of stimuli to our thoughts and feelings. Above all, the congregation itself, whether faces are familiar or not, suggests by its friendly quietness an unseen Presence that draws us into communication with Itself. The character of this Presence is more sharply defined for us by the symbols that surround us and catch our eye. Some of these symbols recall to us, vaguely perhaps, teaching we have received. Others bring back hallowed associations of very distinct experiences with the living God. Distinguished from all other impressions upon us will be a cross—on an altar or a rood beam, or traced in a window or wall, or possibly recalled only to the eye of the mind. But our instinctive reaction to it will be like that of Sir Thomas Browne, in his *Religio Medici*: "At the sight of a cross, or crucifix, I can dispense with my hat, but scarce with the thought or memory of my Saviour."

All these suggestions and impressions have but one purpose—to make us aware of the presence of God. For the beginning and end of all worship is awareness of God. Every form of worship, both in its contents and in its conduct, is a disclosure of God, of His existence and power, His character and His demands. Every thought and word and gesture in worship, whether expressed in silent awe or in choral song, celebrates the majesty of His being, the righteousness of His will, and the unfailing justice and mercy of His dealings with men.

It is God's presence, ever seeking communion with His creatures, ever available to those who seek Him, that sustains and perfects our worship. He is "always more ready to hear than we to pray"; and He is "wont to give more than either we desire or deserve" (Prayer Book, p. 206). God in His love for us always takes the initiative. Hence our worship of Him is best described in terms of our response—the response of creatures to their Maker, the response of sinners to their Redeemer. The famous affirmation of St. Augustine has been the confession of all true worshippers in every generation and place: "Thou hast made us for thyself, and our hearts are restless till they find rest in thee." [1]

God takes the initiative toward us in our worship not only because He loves us, but also because He judges us. The opening psalm of our Morning Prayer forcefully reminds us of this. "He cometh with righteousness to judge the world, and the peoples with his truth." This inescapable certainty of God's judgment, in mercy and in truth, imparts to worship both its necessity and its urgency. It also preserves worship from all pretense and prevarication. In God's sight no man can justify himself. Unto Him "all hearts are open, all desires known," and from Him "no

---

[1] *Confessions* i., 1.

secrets are hid." All of our Lord's teaching about prayer and worship is given us from this perspective. The self-righteous hypocrite received His severest condemnation. For his prayers were a denial of that sincerity and truth demanded by our Father in heaven, who both "seeth in secret" and "knoweth what things we have need of, before we ask him" (Matt. 6:4,6,8,18,32).

ADORATION AND PRAISE

As flowers break forth into blossom from the warmth and nourishment of sun and rain and fertile soil, so adoration and praise spring from our awareness of the sustaining presence of a God who loves us. Adoration is the primary impulse of worship. It is also its chief end and fulfillment. To know God truly, who He is and what He does, in so far as human mind and heart can comprehend Him; to ponder upon His infinite power and wisdom that brought all things that exist into being out of nothing; to contemplate the unsearchable reaches of love that move a hardened sinner to repentance and faith; to glimpse the possibilities of life that issue from obedience to His commandments—to be alive to such presence and power and promise is to adore God.

Adoration and worship are really one and the same thing. Adoration is the frame in which the Church's corporate offices of worship are set. Morning and Evening Prayer open with a psalm of praise and close with a thanksgiving "for all the blessings of this life." The Holy Communion is exactly what its most ancient title implies—a Eucharist, that is to say, a "thanksgiving." It is framed by an opening response, called the Kyrie ("Lord, have mercy upon us"), wherein we acknowledge God's sovereign lordship over us. It closes with this same response in the great doxology, "Glory be to God on high." In the very midst of these services the purest hymn of adoration ever conceived breaks through: the *Sanctus* of the *Te Deum* and the Consecration Prayer:

> Holy, Holy, Holy, Lord God of hosts,
> Heaven and earth are full of thy glory.

We must not think of adoration in our worship solely in terms of the more formal hymns and canticles of praise. Adoration is expressed in many ways and in many forms. Whenever we read the Holy Scriptures or recite the Creeds in our worship we are adoring God. For though these words are read for our edification and profit, they are read no less to the glory of God. They are recitals of His mighty acts for man's redemption, how He has wrought in us and for us that which no man of his own sufficiency and power can do, either for himself or for another.

All the prayers of our common worship are acts of adoration. Almost invariably they open with an ascription of praise. Whether directly in their address to God, or in some qualifying clause, they state an attribute of His nature or describe an aspect of His character and work. These clauses offer us a wealth of material for meditation upon the wonder and love of God's being and activity. To take but one example, in the opening invocation of the baptismal service we read: "Almighty and immortal God, the aid of all who need, the helper of all who flee to thee for succour, the life of those who believe, and the resurrection of the dead" (Prayer Book, p. 274). In the prayers of certain pagan religions, this kind of explicit mention of the deity's attributes was employed in a spirit of bargain: since thou art declared to be of such and such a nature, we expect thee to do such and such for us as a consequence. But in Christian worship the use of these epithets in prayer to describe God's nature and work is no bargain surely, but the loving response of dependent and grateful creatures to One "from whom all holy desires, all good counsels, and all just works do proceed." For we are taught in God's Word that when we ask of Him the things that are good and needful, we ask neither as importunate beggars nor as creditors making a due claim. We ask of Him as adoring children of a Father who is ever ready to give more than we desire or deserve.

In adoring God the Church in its worship becomes a representative voice of God's entire creation, both the visible and the invisible, the animate and the inanimate. Those who have stood on the rim of Grand Canyon and surveyed its solemn grandeur, or who have looked through a magnifying lens at the intricate varieties of microscopic forms of life and matter, know that there are rapturous, though inaudible praises offered to God continually from His whole creation. The Psalmist knew of these praises when he sang of the heavenly bodies:

> There is neither speech nor language;
> but their voices are heard among them.
> Their sound is gone out into all lands;
> and their words into the ends of the world. (19:3-4.)

The Church's worship is one strain of melody in this larger chorus. Our morning canticle *Benedicite* ("O all ye works of the Lord") is perhaps the noblest example of this cosmic frame of our worship (Prayer Book, pp. 11-13). We recall that when the Pharisees asked our Lord to rebuke His disciples for their acclamations of praise to Him as He rode triumphantly into Jerusalem, He replied: "I tell you that, if these should hold their peace, the stones would immediately cry out" (Luke 19:40).

More intimate than our share in the worship of created nature is the linking of our praise with the adoration of God by the invisible choirs of heaven. Again and again the Church's worship enters within the veil that separates the things that are seen from the things that are not seen.

Therefore with Angels and Archangels, and with all the company of heaven, we laud and magnify thy glorious Name; evermore praising thee, and saying, Holy, Holy, Holy. (Prayer Book, p. 77.)

These words are no mystic fantasy or poetic invention, though the language we use to express this reality must of necessity be imaginative and symbolic. We have to do in this aspect of our worship with a revelation made known to us in the visions of seers and prophets and in the devotions of holy and humble men of heart. "In the year that King Uzziah died," the prophet Isaiah heard the angelic *Sanctus* when he saw "the Lord sitting upon a throne, high and lifted up, and his train filled the temple" (Isa. 6:1 ff.). Similarly, the seer of Patmos heard the glad thanksgivings of the martyrs of the Faith, who stand "before the throne of God, and serve him day and night in his temple" (Rev. 7:15). The Bethlehem shepherds received angelic visitors on the night our Saviour Christ was born and listened to their *Gloria in excelsis*.

We, too, presume to lift our hearts to join in heaven's praises. For though we are sinners, unworthy of that company, "we have an Advocate with the Father." By His Ascension our Lord and Saviour has taken our humanity into heaven itself, "now to appear in the presence of God for us" (Heb. 9:24). Because He makes us one with Him, we have access to God. Through Him we have a share in the glory that He offers to the Father eternally, throughout all ages and world without end.[2]

PENITENCE

Although our awareness of God's presence evokes from us the joy of adoration, it also sends us to our knees in humble penitence. Praise and penitence are inseparably linked in worship. Isaiah relates that his own immediate response to his vision of the heavenly, adoring hosts was a confession: "Woe is me! for I am undone; because I am a man of unclean lips." When we are lifted up out of ourselves to behold God's power and love, we are revealed to ourselves at the same time for what we really are. In the presence of God's power we know our own frailty. In the presence of His love we recognize our own selfishness. In the presence of His holiness we confess our own sinfulness.

What is it like to stand in the presence of the holy?
It is like lifting up one's eyes to the hills and knowing their strength and our littleness.
It is like hearing the voice of many waters.
It is like going into a place so clean that one draws back lest he soil that cleanness.
It is like standing in a light before which one must shade his eyes.

---

[2] See *The Faith of the Church*, pp. 102-103.

It is like hearing a rebuke from one you love and knowing it is true and being inwardly smitten.

It is like receiving a gift beyond all expectation and not knowing what to say.

It is like standing before Christ and knowing the glory of his life and the tawdriness of one's own.

It is like all these, but it is not the same as any of these, save standing before Christ, for He is holy.[3]

We must not consider our sense of unworthiness and guilt in God's presence as due to the frailty of our human nature. God does not condemn us because we are creatures of limited capacities and finite strength.

> For he knoweth whereof we are made;
> he remembereth that we are but dust. (Ps. 103:14.)

Nor does He hold us to account for errors of conduct or of judgment that result, not from an evil will, but from lack of available knowledge. Though ignorance is by no means always excusable, certain knowledge is not always attainable. No loving and understanding parent punishes a child for faults that cannot be helped. What puts the shame upon our neglect and disobedience of God is the knowledge that we could have done better under the circumstances, and more than that, the consciousness of having spurned the freely offered assistances of His grace. And among the chief of these assistances is that constant attendance upon His worship, whereby we "may both perceive and know what things we ought to do, and also may have grace and power faithfully to fulfil the same" (Prayer Book, p. 109).

---

[3] Angus Dun, *Not by Bread Alone*, New York: Harpers, 1942, pp. 14-15. (Quoted by permission of the publishers.)

Sin is separation from God. It is the setting of our self-will in place of God's will.[4] Our Prayer Book services, with their emphasis upon the keeping of God's commandments, mislead some people into identifying sin with overt acts of disobedience of God's law. Thus we confess that we have both "left undone those things which we ought to have done; and we have done those things which we ought not to have done" (Prayer Book, pp. 6, 23). But these outward acts of negligence or of disobedience are the result of inward "devices and desires of our hearts." They spring from a lack of love of God and of our neighbor. Where love is absent there is separation and self-isolation. That is the essence of sin. And who can say in God's presence that their love of Him and of their neighbor is enough? In the parable of the Pharisee and the publican (Luke 18:9 ff.) our Lord condemned the prayer of the Pharisee and approved the prayer of the publican. Certainly by any standard of outward conformity to God's law, the Pharisee was a better man than the publican. The Pharisee, however, was self-righteous and without love, being proud of his "separation" from the publican. Hence his prayer was not acceptable. His presumption that God would approve his works of righteousness as sufficient revealed him as a more callous sinner than the penitent publican.

In the psalms, lessons and prayers of our worship we are reminded again and again of the abundance of God's blessings upon us, both material and spiritual. Our imagination is awakened to the almost limitless possibilities of good which we can make of these blessings both in our own lives and in the lives of our fellow men. When St. Paul listed

---

[4] See *The Faith of the Church*, pp. 63 ff.

the fruit of the Spirit—"love, joy, peace, longsuffering, gentleness, goodness, faith, meekness, temperance"— he made the telling comment that "against such there is no law" (Gal. 5:22-23). That is to say, there is no end to the growth of these Christ-like qualities in our lives if we will only surrender ourselves to the inner working of the Holy Spirit. In the face of such bounteous gifts offered us freely and undeservedly we stand before God as miserable sinners indeed. "If ye then, being evil, know how to give good gifts unto your children," said our Lord, "how much more shall your heavenly Father give the Holy Spirit to them that ask him?" (Luke 11:13.) So at the very beginning of our worship, when we ask God's cleansing pardon of our sin, we ask also for the gift of His Spirit.

Wherefore let us beseech him to grant us true repentance, and his Holy Spirit, that those things may please him which we do at this present; and that the rest of our life hereafter may be pure and holy. (Prayer Book, pp. 7, 24.)

Cleanse the thoughts of our hearts by the inspiration of thy Holy Spirit, that we may perfectly love thee, and worthily magnify thy holy Name. (Prayer Book, p. 67.)

When Isaiah discovered his own sinfulness, as he stood in adoration before the presence of the Holy, it was not his own personal sin alone that he felt compelled to confess, but also the sin of his people. "I dwell in the midst of a people of unclean lips" (Isa. 6:5). We can no more escape involvement in the sinfulness of our society than we can suppose that our most personal and secret sins have no social consequences.[5] For we are all members one of

---

[5] *Ibid.*

another, both by our nature and by our redemption in Christ. As we cannot love God without also loving our neighbor, so we cannot sin against God without also defrauding one another. For this reason the Church's prayers always present the confession of sin in the plural. They are *general* confessions, i.e., corporate acts of repentance. And precisely because they are corporate, every Christian, no matter how upright and saintly his personal life may be, can say in utmost sincerity with his brethren the general Confession: "The remembrance of them is grievous unto us; The burden of them is intolerable" (Prayer Book, p. 75).

Over and beyond all other societies, the Church must be sensitive to the evil in the world and its own failure to combat that evil with all its heart and mind and strength. More serious in the sight of God than the evil of the world is the sin within the Church itself—its lack of unity, love and zeal. The Holy Communion is certainly, in the mercy of God, the supreme gift of His love to His Church in its worship. But it is also the most exacting judgment that He lays upon us. We offer the Eucharist as "our sacrifice of praise and thanksgiving"; but at the same time we must admit that "we are unworthy, through our manifold sins, to offer unto thee any sacrifice." Our prayers and oblations are presented to God with the intent that He may "inspire continually the Universal Church with the spirit of truth, unity, and concord . . . that all those who do confess thy holy Name may agree in the truth of thy holy Word, and live in unity and godly love." Yet we offer these intentions of our Eucharist again and again upon the broken tables of a divided Christendom. We present them in the very midst of the prejudices, fears and injustices that hinder the reconciliation of classes, races and nations. We are indeed "not worthy so much as to gather up the crumbs under thy Table." Surely our worship of God in sincerity and truth demands that we accompany without ceasing the adoration of the heavenly *Sanctus* with the earthly *Kyrie eleison,* "Lord, have mercy upon us."

REVELATION

Though the being and purpose of God are disclosed to us in all our praises and prayers of adoration and confession, He is revealed in a very special way in our worship in the reading and preaching of His Word. The use of sacred Scriptures in our Christian worship, as an integral part of our common service, is an inheritance from the Jewish synagogue. And it is no accident that this is so. It accords with the very nature of our Jewish-Christian tradition of faith itself. The God whom we worship is neither an aspect or force of nature, nor is He an invention of legend and myth. He is a living Person who reveals Himself in history in the concrete situations and events of our common life.[6] The Bible is the record of that historical revelation; and in reading and expounding it we come into direct relationship with that revelation. The Bible is the source and fountain of the truth that we believe and the hope by which we live. Without it our worship, no less than our Faith, would wither and die.

The Book of Common Prayer, like other great embodiments of the tradition of Christian worship, is almost entirely composed out of the Scriptures, either directly by

---

[6] See Chapter V; also *The Holy Scriptures* (especially Chapter I), and *The Faith of the Church,* pp. 50-51.

excerpts and quotations from it, or indirectly by allusions to and paraphrases of it. In the daily offices of Morning and Evening Prayer almost the entire contents of the Bible are read in an ordered course throughout each year. Lessons from the Scriptures are appointed for the other offices of the Prayer Book; and there is hardly a prayer in the Book that does not quote some passage of the Bible. In the preface of the first Prayer Book of 1549 it was stated that in this Book "is ordained nothing to be read, but the very pure word of God, the holy scriptures, or that which is evidently grounded upon the same." Certainly no other body of Christian people can claim a worship more agreeable to God's Word than those who use the liturgy of the Prayer Book. The Prayer Book is the Bible itself, ordered and arranged for corporate devotional use.

The Scriptures are read in our worship both as an act of praise to God and as a means of instruction of ourselves. By its teaching and exhortation we are continually advanced and strengthened in our devotion and obedience to God. The lessons of the Bible stir us to repentance and faith in Him, to love of Him and of one another in the household of faith, to concern for those who are without the light and peace of fellowship with our Lord. Thus the reading of the Bible is in itself an act of worship, since it evokes in us the basic attitudes of worship: penitence, thanksgiving, and self-surrender to the will of God. One may read the Scriptures, of course, for other reasons: for historical information, for enjoyment of literature, for proof of doctrine. But these purposes do not preclude, and they even enhance, the worshipful reading of God's Word, if we always read it in the spirit of reverence and humility.

When the Bible is read in public worship it is accompanied by an interpretation. For its religious message is not always readily understood by modern hearers. The books of the Bible were written over the course of many centuries under many different situations and from many different points of view. In the oldest material of the Bible there are primitive expressions of religious belief and practice which in later books are superseded or even contradicted. Precisely because it is an historical record, the Bible tells a story of growth and development in man's knowledge of God and of His purposes for human life. But the Bible has a unity of theme from beginning to end because it is the revelation of the one and only God.[7]

The Church's worship helps us to discover the unity of the Bible and the key to its interpretation. For one thing, it suggests, by the arrangement of the lessons, that the New Testament is the fulfillment of the Old, not only because it was written after the Old Testament but also because it interprets the purpose of the Old Testament. At the Holy Communion the Gospel lesson receives a greater honor than the other lessons of Scripture because Christ is the center and the key of the whole biblical revelation. The word of our Lord Himself is our guarantee of this fact. At the opening of His public ministry, when He stood up in the synagogue at Nazareth to read the Old Testament, He commented upon the lesson thus: "This day is this scripture fulfilled in your ears" (Luke 4:21). When disputing with the Jews He said, "Search the scriptures; for in them ye think ye have eternal life: and they are they which testify of me" (John 5:39). Finally, at the time of His resurrection appearances to His disciples,

[7] See *The Holy Scriptures,* especially Chapter I.

"he expounded unto them in all the scriptures the things concerning himself" (Luke 24:27,44-45).

In the second place, the Church's worship helps us to find the key to interpretation of the Bible by the way the lessons of Scripture are selected. They are chosen for each Sunday and holy day by reason of their appropriateness to the theme of that particular day or season of the Christian Year. Thus two or more lessons, drawn from different parts of the Bible, are given a unity; and their relationship is illuminated by associating them with the thoughts and remembrances of the life and death of our Lord and of His saints. By linking the lesson-theme with the season-theme the liturgy reminds us in still another way that the clue to the Bible is God's supreme revelation of Himself in our Lord Jesus Christ.

The recital of the Creeds in close association with the lessons serves the same interpretive purpose. The Creeds are summaries of the mighty acts of God. They are based upon the apostles' preaching that in Christ God has come into the world "for us men and for our salvation . . . according to the Scriptures." [8] The use of Creeds in our worship is often misunderstood. They are not recited in the liturgy as tests of orthodoxy, to exclude people who have difficulties with their dogmatic statements. Of course, as a matter of history, one of the purposes of the Creeds was to defend the Church from certain heresies. But in the context of worship the Creeds are inclusive, not exclusive. They are positive affirmations of the truth revealed to us in the Holy Scriptures. They are reminders of the promises of faith in God and in His Christ and Holy

---

[8] See *The Faith of the Church,* Chapter I.

Spirit that we made in our Baptism, when we were made members of Christ in His holy Church.[9]

The Word of God is also interpreted for us in our worship by preaching. By preaching, the revelation of God in the Bible is made present and alive in our very midst here and now, in all its grace and judgment and power. By the preacher's word we are enabled to appropriate the Bible's Word to ourselves and apply it to our own present experience. And the focal center of the preacher's word is Christ and His gospel. Preaching is therefore a true form of worship because it brings us into the living presence of God in adoration, in penitence and in self-surrender to Him. It has often been said, and rightly so, that preaching is like a sacrament. It is a means whereby the redeeming love of God in Christ is continually given and received in His Church. True preaching is far more than a moving and inspiring address. It is nothing less than the living God acting through the voice of His prophets to bring His people to salvation and redemption. A great theologian of our time has described the sacramental character of preaching thus:

The preacher, in reproducing this Gospel word of God, prolongs Christ's sacramental work. The real presence of Christ crucified is what makes preaching. It is what makes of a speech a sermon, and of a sermon Gospel. This is the work of God, this continues His work in Christ, that ye should believe in Him whom He hath sent . . . The preacher's word, when he preaches the gospel and not only delivers a sermon, is an effective deed, charged with blessing or with judgment. We eat and drink judgment to ourselves as we hear. It is not an utterance,

[9] See Chapter VIII. For the history of the Creeds, see *Chapters in Church History,* pp. 33-36. Cf. *The Faith of the Church,* pp. 22-24.

and not a feat, and not a treat. It is a sacramental act, done together with the community in the name and power of Christ's redeeming act and our common faith. It has the real presence of the active Word whose creation it is.[10]

PETITION, INTERCESSION, AND OFFERING

A constant element in the Church's corporate worship has been its prayers of petition and intercession, for ourselves and for all men, for "those things which are requisite and necessary, as well for the body as the soul" (Prayer Book, pp. 6, 23). Certain subjects of intercession are found in all the principal offices of corporate worship in the Prayer Book—the State and its rulers, the Church and its ministry, the unity of God's people and the mission of the Gospel, and all those who in any way need "succour, help, and comfort" by reason of their being "in danger, necessity, and tribulation" (Prayer Book, p. 56). Included in these general supplications are all the particular and specific intentions of our immediate time and circumstance. For in the perspective of our "common" prayer our private, personal requests must lose all selfish concern and be related to the larger good of our common life.

Yet there is no element of our worship more commonly misunderstood, certainly none is more commonly misrepresented, than our prayers of petition and intercession. Some people consider them unnecessary. Since God knows our needs better than we do, He will supply them in His good providence when it is fitting and proper in His sight to do so. It is presuming upon His knowledge and kindness to remind Him of our necessities. For other people, pray-

[10] P. T. Forsyth, *Positive Preaching and Modern Mind,* New York: A. C. Armstrong and Son, 1908, pp. 82-83.

ers of petition and intercession are a superstitious kind of magic. Such prayers, they say, are an unwarranted attempt to interfere with God's unchangeable laws. What is worse, they are devices to bend God's will to ours. Such views as these, though they are sincerely held by conscientious persons, are nonetheless the result of misconceptions about the nature of God, His relation to the world He has made, and the way He deals with men. They are contrary to our Lord's express teaching, and to the spirit of the Prayer which He taught His disciples, the "Our Father."

It is indeed true that God knows "our necessities before we ask, and our ignorance in asking." It is also true that God bestows upon us many blessings "which for our unworthiness we dare not, and for our blindness we cannot ask" (Prayer Book, pp. 49-50). But in many instances, God waits for us to ask of His grace. For He wants us to know and recognize for ourselves what is good for us, to be eager to have what is good, and to be ready to use His gifts properly and beneficially. But to know what is good for us and how to use His gifts rightly, we must relate our requests to the ultimate purposes which God seeks. Our petitions must have the breadth of His perspective. A phrase in one of the Prayer Book collects states the condition laid upon our prayers thus: "That they may obtain their petitions, make them to ask such things as shall please thee" (p. 203). And that is nothing less than the advancement and final achievement of His Kingdom. The gifts and graces that we ask of God must contribute to the coming of His Kingdom "on earth as it is in heaven."

Our petitions and intercessions must be of one piece with our adoration of God's righteous will and loving purpose. The more God's inexhaustible concern for the good of His creatures takes possession of our own hearts and minds, the more nearly shall our requests conform to His saving intention and work. "The object of prayer," said Bishop Gore, "is not to bring the divine will down to the human, but to lift the human up into correspondence with the divine." [11] We must have ever before us the example of our Lord's life of prayer: "Not what I will, but what thou wilt" (Mark 14:36).

But this is exactly the point where our selfishness and sin enter in. Whatever we ask of God, we must ask penitently. For we are constantly asking for blessings that we are not spiritually prepared to have. Whether we admit it or not we are thinking more of our own satisfaction than of the advancement of God's glory. For example, we pray day after day for peace. But we do not get peace, because the only true peace is "that peace which is the fruit of righteousness." Our righteousness is not nearly enough. There is pride and envy and fear in our own hearts. There is greed and injustice and vainglory in our society. There is distrust and hypocrisy and malice in our international relations. If God gave us peace, what would we do with it? Would we enrich ourselves, exploit the underprivileged, and dominate the weak? Or would we show forth in our lives what the Lord requires of us: namely, "to do justly, and to love mercy, and to walk humbly with thy God" (Micah 6:8)? On our answers to these questions depends God's answer to our prayers, whether He says yes or no.

There are, to be sure, mysteries in prayer which we

---

[11] Charles Gore, *The Sermon on the Mount*, 3rd ed., New York: E. P. Dutton and Co., 1912, p. 150.

cannot fathom. There are blessings which we seek for ourselves and for others that we believe in all good faith are in accord with God's will and love. Yet they are delayed, or they are not given. We ask for rain upon a dry and thirsty earth that it may yield its increase to our material relief. We intercede for one who is wracked with pain and torment, that he may be restored to health of body and mind. How the natural evils of dearth, decay and death fit into the total purpose of God we cannot certainly know in this life. What we do know is that God's love and gifts are to be sought, as they are given, in the way that is most profitable for us. His gifts of the Spirit, love, joy, peace, etc., are far more important for us to have than the material blessings of health and wealth, or even life itself. For "a man's life consisteth not in the abundance of the things [i.e., material things] which he possesseth" (Luke 12:15). It consists in those qualities of character that can make the poor man generous and given to hospitality, the sick man full of cheer and thankfulness, the bereaved man unshaken in faith and hope.

In the last analysis all our prayers of petition and intercession are acts of self-oblation, the free offering and surrender of our finite and imperfect love into the hands of God's infinite and almighty love. The Church's prayer prevails only to the extent of its responsive offering of itself to God to be the instrument of His will. Worship is consummated in offering. And its offering must be total and entire. God so loved that He *gave*—gave us nothing less than Himself in His only-begotten Son Jesus Christ. Our adoring and penitent response to His love is the offering of ourselves and of all the love of which we are capable by the help of His grace. It is a great pity that so many people think of the "offering" in worship solely in terms of a collection of money. But our "alms and oblations" of material gifts are intimately associated with our prayers and intercessions.[12] They are the partial, outward tokens of a complete, inward dedication to His service of everything that we are and everything that we possess, both our material and our spiritual gifts.

When we describe worship as consummated in offering, we are saying that worship is sacrifice. The word " sacrifice" literally means "to make sacred." It is positive, not negative in meaning. Sacrifice is not the *giving up* of a costly possession, possibly to the point of losing life itself. It is the *giving over* of all that we are and have into the keeping of Him who is Himself the Giver of every good and perfect gift. We give over to God ourselves, our talents and our possessions for Him to make them sacred, to sanctify them to His use. God in turn restores these gifts to us in Holy Communion—cleansed, perfected and empowered by His love. And thus we are enabled to share them one with another in fellowship and service according to His will.

THROUGH JESUS CHRIST OUR LORD

Our offering, however, is never perfect, never entire. It always bears the stain of our selfishness and our sin. How then can God accept it? In so far as it is sinful it is not pleasing to Him. But He does accept it even so. He receives it from our hands and hearts for Christ's sake. In Jesus Christ alone our humanity realized perfectly the full obedience of prayer: "Not what I will, but what thou wilt." Through Christ alone our humanity is enabled to

---

[12] See Chapter VII for the meaning of the Offertory.

present its feeble prayers and imperfect offerings as an acceptable worship before the divine Majesty. Hence all our prayer and all our praise is addressed to God in Christ's Name.

It is these five words, "through Jesus Christ our Lord," that impart to Christian worship its unique and distinctive character. For His Name is written over everything we do in common prayer. We make confession of our sins and plead for God's forgiveness for Christ's sake. We praise Him above all things for His redemption of the world through our Lord Jesus Christ. We send up our petitions and intercessions for ourselves and for others in Christ's Name. We offer the service of our lives for Christ's glory. The loving communion between God and man that all worship seeks is possible only through the mediation of Jesus Christ, who is both God and man. "And this is the confidence that we have in him, that if we ask any thing according to his will, he heareth us: and if we know that he hear us, whatsoever we ask, we know that we have the petitions that we desired of him" (1 John 5:14-15).

CHAPTER THREE

Liturgical Worship

IN THE YEAR 1689, when James II was driven from the English throne and succeeded by William and Mary, an unseemly controversy was raging on this side of the Atlantic in Puritan Boston. The efforts of the royal governor of Massachusetts to introduce the public celebration of the Prayer Book services were stoutly resisted by the leading Puritan divines. One of their most notable ministers, Increase Mather, published a scurrilous pamphlet entitled *A Brief Discourse Concerning the Unlawfulness of the Common Prayer Worship.*

Mather's book described the liturgy of the Church of England as little short of idolatrous, and declared that some things in it "cannot be practised without sin." The services of the Prayer Book were called "broken Responds and shreds of Prayer which the Priests and People toss between them like Tennis Balls." It was no less than "an Apostacy," said he, "in this Age of Light to countenance or comply with the Common Prayer-Book worship. A stinted Liturgy is opposite to the Spirit of Prayer." And he went on to add, "I would not forget those Eminent and Faithful Ministers of Christ who were driven into an American desert, the principal cause of whose Exile, and

Sufferings, was because they durst not touch with the Common Prayer-Book." [1]

We may smile today at these quaint and bitter words. But they remind us in a vivid way of a long-standing division in English and American Christianity, stemming from the age of the Reformation, between those Christians who use a liturgical form of corporate worship and those who spurn all the formalities of written prayers and read service.

The objections of the Puritans to the use of the Prayer Book stemmed from various motives. One of them was a deep-seated prejudice against anything even remotely related to the worship of the Roman Catholic Church. It is, of course, an indisputable fact that the Book of Common Prayer is a direct descendant of the Latin rites of medieval Catholicism. The Puritans also objected to some of the doctrines expressed in the prayers of the Book. And some of the ceremonies prescribed in the Book, such as the sign of the cross in Baptism and the giving of a ring in Holy Matrimony, they viewed as little less than outright superstition. Underlying all their criticism of its use, however, was a basic principle which they believed to be derived from the teaching of the New Testament: "Quench not the Spirit; despise not prophesyings." A prescribed, written order of worship seemed to the Puritan a denial of the inspiration of the Holy Spirit, promised to all who would pray according to the mind of God.

Many devout Christians still share these Puritan sentiments against "liturgical" services. They consider such

[1] For the details of this controversy, see W. S. Perry, *The History of the American Episcopal Church,* 1587-1883, Vol. I, Boston: James R. Osgood and Co., 1885, pp. 175 ff.

worship overly formal and external in character, a fixed, routine sort of thing lacking in freedom, simplicity and naturalness of expression. Oftentimes they associate liturgical worship with an elaborate use of symbolism and ceremony culled from the hoary past, and a strange kind of music called chanting that sounds like nothing else in this world. These impressions, however, are the result of a misunderstanding about the essential nature of a liturgy. Outward adornments do not make a liturgy, any more than clothes make a man. A congregation assembled in a richly ornamented cathedral does not worship liturgically if it only listens mutely to a minister reading prayers and a choir singing chants, however exquisitely they may be rendered. What then is the root meaning of "liturgy"?

THE MEANING OF LITURGY

The word liturgy, like so many technical terms of religion, has a secular origin. It comes to us from the Greeks, who formed the term out of two words meaning "people" and "work." When a citizen of ancient Athens paid at his own expense for a public work or entertainment, or supplied equipment for the armed forces, he was said to have performed a liturgy. Sometimes this office was voluntary; at other times it was imposed on wealthy citizens by the State.

In the Greek version of the Old Testament (the Septuagint) this non-religious use of the word liturgy is occasionally found. More commonly it was used to describe the ministries performed by the priests and Levites in the temple. So we find the word employed in the New Testament to denote the duties discharged by Zacharias, the father of John the Baptist (Luke 1.13). St. Paul used the term in various contexts. In one place he applied it to the civil magistrates: they were ministers, i.e., *liturgists,* of God (Rom. 13:6). He also described himself as "the *liturgist* of Jesus Christ to the Gentiles, ministering (i.e., performing the sacred *hierurgy,* or *liturgy,* of) the Gospel of God, that the offering of the Gentiles might be acceptable, being sanctified by the Holy Ghost" (Rom. 15:16). In the Book of Acts the prophets and teachers at Antioch are spoken of as *liturgizing* to the Lord, i.e., leading the Church's public worship (13:2).

In the course of time the early Christians came to restrict the word liturgy to the public functions of the Church presided over by its official ministers. In the Eastern Orthodox Churches the word became a technical title used solely to denote the rite of the Eucharist. St. Benedict of Nursia described the liturgy of his monks, namely their corporate acts of worship, as "the work of God," and deemed it the most important activity of the religious community.

Thus in its root meaning, liturgy means an act performed for the good of a community. In its commonly restricted meaning, it refers to the public rites and ceremonies officially authorized by the Church, in contrast to the private prayers and devotions of individuals or of voluntary groups of Christians. It is literally the "work of the people" in their common life of prayer. It involves a responsible and active participation by all the worshippers, the congregation no less than the ministers. Though he meant it for a jibe, Increase Mather was not far off the mark when he described the Prayer Book liturgy as "Prayer which the Priests and People toss between them like Tennis Balls." For the players on both sides of the net have their turn in "serving."

Liturgical worship has frequently been compared to a drama. But the analogy is not quite exact. In a theater a small company of players perform before an audience. The audience may be profoundly moved or delightfully entertained by the actors. But it has no responsibility for the drama. In a liturgy, however, all the assembly are the players, and each one must know his lines and his cues. The more familiar a player's part, the more ready he is to carry on the drama with understanding and with zest. We shall see in a later chapter how the requirements of liturgical worship have influenced the development in the Church of orders of ministry. For the bishop, the presbyter, the deacon, and the layman, each has his own order or function in the drama of the liturgy.

Because liturgical worship demands a corporate participation, it is easy to see how liturgies tend to become fixed in the use of habitual and familiar forms. Such forms may be "frozen" by being written down; or they may be transmitted by an oral tradition. Though it is possible to worship liturgically without employing old or familiar phrases, most liturgies in use among Christians do have a traditional cast and an ancient pedigree. But liturgies are constantly undergoing revision and alteration. The service books found among the several Churches of Christendom reveal the hands of many men of many different times and places, some of them known, many of them unknown. New liturgical usages are constantly being invented to enrich, to modify, or even to supplant older ones. In the next chapter we shall trace the story of how the rites of the Book of Common Prayer have come down to us through the centuries. Meanwhile, it will be helpful to analyze the various elements which go to make up a liturgical office of worship.

THE ELEMENTS OF LITURGICAL WORSHIP

Every liturgy consists of three elements: order, ritual, and ceremonial. These elements are to be found in all liturgies, but they occur in various combinations of elaborateness or of fixity.

1. *Order.* The order of a liturgy is its structural framework, its shape and design. It must be invariable. For without a fixed order a liturgy is like a body without a skeleton, a game without rules. A fixed order is necessary if worship is to be corporate. People must know what to expect, what comes next. If they do not know the order they cannot be active participants. Instead they become passive receivers of their leader's private devotions. But as we have already seen, a liturgy is not a personal exercise of devotion performed in public, however helpful and instructive such a form of worship might be. Liturgy involves the give and take of minister and people. It can have this corporate character only when all the participants know where and when their respective parts come in the service.

Frequently the order of a liturgy is determined by a logic inherent in the ceremonies that have to be performed. The water in the font must be blessed before the candidate is baptized in it. The bread and wine are first taken, then blessed, then distributed in communion. Any other arrangement would be illogical. Not all designs in liturgies are so obvious. For example, should penitence lead to praise, or should the act of adoration precede and suggest penitence? In the previous chapter we have already noted that adoration and penitence are almost simultaneous responses to the presence of God. Again, should our intercessions at the Eucharist be associated with our offerings, or with the consecration of these offerings, or with our communion?

Such questions have no ready-made answers. The various liturgies of the Churches of Christendom solve them in different ways. But any well-ordered liturgy has its own principle of arrangement, its own rhythm of movement and of progress. This is what we call the *rationale* of a liturgy. At its best a liturgy will make sense, both logically and psychologically. It will have a reason for its shape and design. When we discuss the services of the Prayer Book, in Part II, we shall try to analyze this inherent reason or order in each of its several offices.

2. *Ritual.* Ritual is the vocal organ of a liturgy, the words that are said or sung. It states and interprets the meaning of what the worshippers do together. Christian worship is, above everything else, a communication of words—of God's Word to men and of man's words to God. It is a special means whereby God's Word of grace and of judgment is proclaimed. "Faith cometh by hearing," said St. Paul, "and hearing by the word of God" (Rom. 10:17). It is true that worship can be real and effective, even in a corporate way, without any word. The silence of the Quaker meeting is proof of this. Many a Catholic, too, has known the communication of God's presence, in company with his fellows, silently on his knees at a Low Mass, when he has neither heard nor understood a single word uttered by the priest. But this has been possible only because the Word of truth has been communicated to him

at some other time in some other way. For it is the Word that imparts meaning to the symbol and the ceremony.

The ritual word is uttered in many ways—in prayers and songs, in reading and in preaching. To communicate the Word a liturgy uses all the arts of rhetoric and of music. For both the spoken and the sung word are different ways, each with its own peculiar kind of expressiveness, of uttering and hearing the truth of God. The hymns, the chants, the anthems and cantatas are lessons and sermons in song. In the same service the same text may be used both for the sermon and the anthem. Yet the same truth is communicated, though with a different effect.

Music has always been married to ritual in liturgical worship. For music is a universal means of expressing feeling and emotion, whether of joy or sorrow, of hope or despair. Because worship involves the whole man, not only his mind but also his emotions, it is only natural that it should express itself in song. And music also has a strange power of binding men and women together in community, for it makes them of one heart and of one voice. It has been said, not without a large measure of truth, that the vitality of the sense of fellowship in a congregation at worship can be judged by the heartiness of its singing. Every revivalist knows that one of the surest ways of melting the stubborn, selfish heart to love for God and the brotherhood is to get the sinner to join in the singing.

It is a mistake, however, to think that there is any specific style of music that is properly liturgical. The splendid liturgy of the Jewish temple was accompanied, as we know from the Psalms, with trumpets, cymbals, strings, and pipe. It must indeed have been a joyful noise unto the Lord. Yet the medieval monastic choir employed no instruments in its liturgy, nor any harmonies, but only the pure, serene melodies of plainsong. Music is liturgical in character not because of its style, but by the effective way it expresses the meaning of the sacred text. It is music married to words, so that they take hold of the worshipper's whole being and lift it up to God. Music rendered for its own sake, as music, however fine it may be, is not properly liturgical. Music has no place in worship if it is designed to entertain or to call attention to itself. Its fitness must be judged by its power to communicate the Word, illumining the mind to truth and strengthening the will to holy obedience and charity.

Whether a service is said or sung, or whether some parts of it are sung and not others, depends upon the tastes and the capacities of a congregation. There is certainly no doctrinal significance to a sung service. One sometimes meets with the curious prejudice that a choral office is "Catholic" while a said service is "Protestant." As a matter of fact the ancient custom of the Church, still preserved in the Eastern Churches, was to consider the choral service as normative. It was the medieval Latin Church that invented the said service, such as Low Mass. This innovation was, to some extent, the making of a virtue out of a necessity; for in small parishes there were not resources available for a fully choral rendering of the liturgy. At the time of the Protestant Reformation, Cranmer employed the famous musician, John Merbecke, to set the Prayer Book services to simple, congregational music.[2] Luther

---

[2] Merbecke's setting of the Holy Communion may be found in the Hymnal, 1940, Nos. 701-707. A recording of this service, and other materials in the Hymnal, under the auspices of the Joint Commission on Church Music, is *Music of the Liturgy in English According to the Use of the Episcopal Church* (Columbia Masterworks, ML 4528).

also provided for the continuance of the choral service; and Calvin engaged the best musicians available for setting the Psalms to appropriate tunes. In certain large churches it is necessary to intone a service if the words are to be heard distinctly by the congregation. What is not properly liturgical, either in Catholic or Protestant Churches, is for the singing of the people's part of the liturgy to be usurped by the choir, or, in some cases, even by the minister.

In all liturgies there are certain parts of the ritual text that belong to the people—responses, creeds, hymns such as the *Sanctus,* or the *Gloria.* There are also specific places where a choir of trained singers may properly minister to the worship of the whole by special chants or anthems of their own. When congregations encourage or permit a choir to take over their own responses and hymns by elaborate musical settings beyond the reach of the average worshipper, they are forfeiting their privileges and responsibilities. They no longer participate in a liturgy; they are listening to a performance.

The ritual element of a liturgy tends, over a period of time, to become fixed and invariable, even the parts assigned to a single minister. This has not always been true. In the early centuries the celebrant at the Eucharist composed the consecration prayer over the bread and wine according to his own inspiration and ability.[3] Only by the fourth century did it become customary for the celebrant to follow fixed and written forms. When a ritual is consolidated in prescribed texts, it does not necessarily lose colorful variety. The prayers, lessons and chants may vary from Sunday to Sunday, from feast day to fast day. The develop-

---

[3] See Chapter IV, pp. 74-75.

ment of the Christian Year, and the adaptation of the liturgy to its themes, have prevented the great historic rites of the Church from falling into a lifeless monotony. In the Prayer Book rites, whether of the daily offices of Morning and Evening Prayer or of the Holy Communion, some parts are fixed and unalterable, other parts vary with the season of the Church Year. Within certain limits, such as the hymns and anthems or prayers connected with the sermon, the Prayer Book allows free, unprescribed choices.

3. *Ceremonial.* Inasmuch as liturgy is always a corporate action, it requires some amount of ceremony. Ceremonial includes the things that are done in worship. The sacraments, at any rate, have to be performed. They involve certain necessary motions and gestures, implements and symbols. Thus the basis of all ceremonial is utilitarian —to do reverently and efficiently what has to be done. But ceremonies may also be interpretive and expressive. The sign of the cross, the bow of the head or the knee, the mixture of wine and water in the chalice, are all meaningful expressions of religious attitudes and beliefs, even though they may not be accompanied by any ritual text that explains them.

Ceremonial includes not only the actions of the ministers but also of the congregation. In some ceremonies all the worshippers take part. For example, all stand to hear the Gospel read at the Eucharist, all make an offering, all kneel at the altar rail to receive communion. In other ceremonies the actions are performed by representatives of the congregation or by the ministers; namely, those who read the lessons, those who present the alms of the people, those who serve the priest at the altar. Of all ceremonies perhaps the most dramatic is the procession. Some processions are necessary, such as the bringing of the gifts to the altar. Others are symbolic, such as wedding processions, or the hymn-singing processions on great festivals—a sort of sacred parade on a gala day, full of the joy and exuberant good spirits that the festival invokes. It should be remembered that processions were not intended to be watched but to be joined. The more people there are in a procession the more meaningful it becomes.

The visual aids of worship are generally included as belonging to ceremonial—the architectural setting, the furnishings and ornaments of the place of worship. Though these may be reduced to the barest essentials, they need not be lacking in beauty and expressiveness. The materials used, the proportions of length and breadth and height of the enclosed space, the design of the holy Table, font and pulpit, the craftsmanship of the sacred vessels for communion—all these can be of such satisfying beauty that they both suggest and express the presence of the holy and invisible God.

The setting of the liturgy may also be richly decorated and include a wealth of symbol carved in wood or stone, or exhibited in painting and colored glass, in vestments and lights. The symbolism may be so rich in suggestion and instruction that many hours can be spent in meditation upon its various, detailed subjects. Ceremonies, too, belong among the visual aids of worship, since we see them as well as do them. Indeed, the deaf and the dumb hear the Word of God only through the language of signs.

Ceremonial is thus intimately related to **art**. Hence ceremonial styles reflect the artistic styles prevailing in the successive generations of history. The cut of a vestment, the size and shape of a font or an altar, the ornament and decoration of a church, are obvious examples of the accepted art-forms of the period when they were made. But ceremonial gestures of reverence, such as standing, bowing, genuflecting, etc., also reflect the good manners of the age in which their use in church was introduced. The ceremonial practices that are acceptable to a congregation depend in large measure upon their artistic tastes, no less than upon familiar custom.

It is certainly true, of course, that some ceremonies are designed to express theological beliefs. At least they are commonly accepted as such. But the unhappy controversies that arise in the Church from time to time over ceremonial are much more the result of differences in taste or custom than they are indications of differences in doctrine. Taste is a fickle thing. We can educate it, but we cannot always control it. For it involves our emotions as well as our minds. But if we are careful to distinguish our differences of taste and custom from our convictions about the truth of our faith, we shall be more tolerant of ceremonial variation in the Church.

As fashions of dress change from age to age, so do ceremonies. We could illustrate this endlessly, but it may suffice to note the changing position of the altar and the ministers in the successive periods of the Church's history. In ancient times the altar was a wooden or stone table, set in front of the sanctuary or even in the midst of the nave. The celebrant and his assistants took their places behind the altar and faced the people. In the Middle Ages the table-altars came to be enclosed on all four sides, taking somewhat the shape of a tomb inasmuch as they enshrined the relics of a saint. They were placed against the east wall of the sanctuary, and the celebrating clergy and servers stood on the same side of the altar as the congregation, facing the same way.

After the Reformation in England these medieval altars were either broken up or abandoned. At the Communion a simple table was placed in the midst of the choir or the body of the church. The minister conducted the service from "the north side." At a later time it became customary for a huge pulpit to dominate the sanctuary; and the holy Table, when there was no Communion, was kept out of sight behind it. When the Gothic style of architecture was revived in the nineteenth century, the medieval arrangements of altar and sanctuary came back into general use. Most Episcopal churches today exhibit this medieval usage. But there is a growing tendency in our own day to return to something like the ancient pattern, with the altar set out from the sanctuary wall so that the minister may again face the people when he leads the Eucharist.

It would be absurd to insist that these varying arrangements of the holy Table and the ministers at the altar indicate any great differences of doctrine. It may be that the ancient custom emphasizes the fellowship-aspect of the Eucharist, whereas the medieval style stresses its sacrificial character. Yet both usages set forth the Eucharist as both a communion and a sacrifice. The difference is primarily one of taste. As in music, so in architecture, there is no one specific style that can be called liturgical. Any style of architecture is appropriate to liturgical worship if its arrangements assist corporate participation in an efficient and meaningful way.

Historic liturgies vary a great deal in respect to how much ceremonial they prescribe, how much they allow, and how much they forbid. The service books of the Roman Church give rather full and detailed directions of ceremonial. But the Prayer Book has very few directions. It usually tells us when to stand, when to sit, when to kneel —though not always. Here and there the minister is directed to turn and face the people, or to cover the sacred vessels of the Communion. Most of the ceremonial witnessed in Episcopal churches, however, is not specified in the Prayer Book. It is a matter of traditional ways of doing things.

Some people are startled to learn, for example, that in no place does the Prayer Book say anything about the colors that we commonly associate with the seasons of the Christian Year. The only place where vestments of any kind are mentioned is in the rite of Consecration of Bishops. Nor does the Prayer Book say *how* the bread and wine for the Communion are to be prepared and presented at the altar. It only tells us *when* they are to be offered. The ceremony of cleansing the sacred vessels after the Communion is nowhere described in the Prayer Book; yet in some churches it is a most elaborate and time-consuming affair. Many choirs do not know that the Prayer Book never speaks of "processionals" and "recessionals"!

The fact that the Prayer Book does not dot the i's and cross the t's of ceremonial explains why there is so much variation of ceremonies from parish to parish in the Episcopal Church. It also explains why so many people confuse ceremony (prescribed actions) and ritual (prescribed texts). A liturgy may have an elaborate ritual with little ceremonial, or a complicated ceremonial with a minimum of ritual. Morning Prayer, for example, is a highly ritualistic office, but it needs very little ceremony for its due and proper performance. Similarly, the Litany may be read without any action at all. But it may also be sung in procession. One should avoid describing a liturgy as very "ritualistic," when what is meant is that it has a rich and colorful ceremonial. The worship of the Episcopal Church, if judged by the Prayer Book alone, is ritualistic to a great degree. That is because the words used in its worship are almost entirely prescribed. But its worship is not highly ceremonious, unless it is made so by the choice and taste of the worshipping congregation.

SACRAMENTAL WORSHIP

Throughout the ages the Church has used a wealth of symbolism in word and gesture and material object to convey the meaning of its faith. Its worship, too, has used these externals. For common worship, like other common activities, requires bodily signs, whether to the eye or the ear or the touch or to all of our senses together. If we ask why this is so, we can only answer that man is made that way. He is not a pure spirit. He is spirit and body. And he uses bodily signs and postures to incite the invisible and hidden workings of his mind and spirit.

At the heart of the Church's common worship are certain signs and symbols that have been given to it with a special grace, a grace expressly promised of God. These are the sacraments. Unlike other signs, sacraments are actual instruments of grace. They convey the very grace they signify. Moreover, we are commanded to do them, and no Church can claim to be part of Christ's Body which neglects or dispenses with the sacraments.

The common prayer of Christians may or may not be liturgical in form. But sacramental worship is always liturgical in character, because the sacraments require for their performance both a given set of corporate actions and an agreed set of interpretive words. They cannot be celebrated by an individual alone, for they have no meaning apart from the community to which they have been given. A man does not baptize himself. He baptizes another, or is himself baptized by another. Baptism is initiation into a fellowship. Similarly, one cannot celebrate the Holy Communion all by oneself. The very word communion connotes sharing and the relationship of persons.

The external signs of the sacraments are given us by our Lord's institution of them.[4] Their material elements, and the words most intimately associated with these elements, are fixed. They are not subject to the whim of the moment. An individual cannot arbitrarily change them by some sudden inspiration. The sacraments are not his; they are the corporate possession of the whole body of the faithful. The baptizer must use water. He cannot dispense with it or properly use anything else. He must baptize in the Name of the Trinity, not in any name he chooses. The bread and the wine are unalterable elements of the Eucharist. And these elements must be identified in some way with the Body and Blood of the Lord.

Thus whenever the Church celebrates the sacraments it performs a liturgy. It engages in a corporate action that has a prescribed form, an essential ritual, and a necessary ceremony. It may elaborate the "given" essentials into a service that lasts for hours. Or it may keep the action to the minimum of what is necessary, as when a priest baptizes or administers communion to a dying man, where the entire service takes only a few minutes. But in both in-

---

[4] See *The Faith of the Church,* pp. 146-47.

stances, whether long or short, rich or bare, it is doing a liturgy, "the work of the people" of God.

VALUES OF A LITURGY

Our analysis of the elements of liturgical worship should help us to answer the Puritan objection that it "quenches the Spirit." To be honest, we must admit that a liturgy can become for some people so formal and external that it ceases to express either their convictions or their feelings. It can be performed in a cut-and-dried manner that is little short of hypocrisy. It can mean no more than what one wag called "reading the minutes of the last meeting." In his novel *The Last Puritan,* George Santayana expressed this deadly externalism in a remark which his character Jim Darnley made about the Prayer Book liturgy: "lovely, sweet channel through which to pour out your feelings, not personal enough to be blushy and not committing you to a single damned dogma."

Yet the abuse of a thing is no argument against it. If a man does not pray his liturgy with sincere devotion the fault may very well be with him rather than with the form of words he is saying. Moreover the fervent prayers "in the Spirit" of a minister who disdains the use of a liturgy may be just as routine, just as unreal, just as unconvincing, to the congregation who listens to him. The real question is not whether the prayers used in worship are freely composed by those who pray or are the written words of an ancient service book. The fundamental thing is whether or not the words of prayer and praise are uttered in sincerity and truth.

Not every Christian, not even every clergyman, has such skill and imagination that he can frame at any given moment a suitable expression of the devotion of a group. One of the chief values of a liturgy is that it teaches us both how to pray and what things we should pray for. It is indeed a means whereby "the Spirit also helpeth our infirmities: for we know not what we should pray for as we ought" (Rom. 8:26). A liturgy disciplines our prayers, making them apt in expression, unselfish in content, and comprehensive in scope. It recalls to us and instructs us in the totality of the Christian faith and in the whole range of worship: confession, praise, intercession and self-offering. Moreover, it is a form of love for our neighbor. For it makes it possible for us to pour out our deepest feelings without trespass upon his legitimate privacy. By joining with him in a common sentiment we do not impose upon him our personal sentimentalities.

Speaking of the Prayer Book collects, Canon William Bright, himself the author of several collects in our liturgy, said,

The careful selection of words, the artistic adjustment of clauses, the melodies which haunt the ear and live in the heart, the force which comprehends so much in so little . . . these fulfil an important function in what may be called the education of the human spirit. They satisfy the sense of religious beauty; they stock the mind with holy memories; . . . they hint at the vastness of Divine truth in comparison with man's attempts to speak of it; they make the soul's conscious approaches to God more steadily reverent, and therefore more healthily real.[5]

A liturgy is most truly a factor in "the education of the human spirit." Perhaps no two persons in any given con-

---

[5] From an essay in *Prayer-Book Commentary for Teachers and Students,* London: S.P.C.K., n.d., pp. 95-96.

gregation are advanced to the same degree of spiritual discernment and experience. Some phrases of a liturgy mean more to one, others to another. It is no hypocrisy to join in a prayer which we do not fervently feel because it has not yet become our own spiritual possession. For it may become ours if we press on with sincere perseverance. A liturgy should teach us to be patient, to be tolerant of aspirations not fully understood or felt. It must stretch our minds and spirits, not only for our own growth but also for our own sympathy for the brotherhood of the faithful.

If a liturgy does anything, it sets our own personal prayers in a large perspective. For it relates them to the whole Church, not merely the visible congregation present, but also the larger company of all the people of God in all ages and climes. Liturgical worship gives us a long-range view, as deep as all the centuries of Christian devotion, as vast as the coming of the Kingdom of God. It is a means of entering into our inheritance of the "communion of saints."

Liturgical worship is not the creation of any individual. It is the product of the whole society or body of which Christ is the Head. It is the folk-worship of those who are "knit together in one communion and fellowship." Participation in it is the giving up of self to the purpose for which that fellowship exists—that by the inspiration of the Holy Spirit, we may perfectly love God and worthily magnify His holy Name. Because the liturgy is the creation of the Church, it is in very truth the creation of the Holy Spirit. The Spirit speaks through it and acts within it. Certainly the activity of the Holy Spirit is not confined to the liturgy or bound by its forms and usages. But He has brought it into being "that he may direct and rule us according to [his] will, comfort us in all our afflictions, defend us from all error, and lead us into all truth" (Prayer Book, p. 183).

According to the Gospel records the only thing the disciples asked our Lord to teach them was how to pray. He did so by giving them a form of words. He did not give it to them merely as a personal, private devotion. It is addressed to *our*, not *my* Father. The Lord's Prayer is a common ritual, a liturgy. Throughout all generations we Christians have repeated its phrases day after day. Yet we never tire of it. Least of all do we ever exhaust the riches of its compact, simple, searching phrases. But the Spirit "helpeth our infirmities" when we say it, teaching us how we should pray it as we ought, until some day when He shall bring us to its final fulfillment, when God's will shall be done on earth as it is in heaven.

CHAPTER FOUR

The Heritage of the Liturgy

IN THE AGE of Queen Elizabeth the great de-
fender of Anglican principles against Puritan
dissent, Richard Hooker, wrote thus of our liturgical heritage:

> . . . the Church hath evermore held a prescript form of
> common prayer, although not in all things every where the
> same, yet for the most part retaining still the same analogy. So
> that if the liturgies of all ancient churches throughout the
> world be compared amongst themselves, it may be easily per-
> ceived they had all one original mould, and that the public
> prayers of the people of God in churches thoroughly settled
> did never use to be voluntary dictates proceeding from any
> man's extemporal wit.[1]

Hooker's claim that the liturgy of the English Church had
an ancient pedigree, deriving from "one original mould,"
is not an exaggeration. The title page of the Book of Common Prayer makes the same appeal, as enshrining the
"Rites and Ceremonies of the Church." It is no less than
the tradition of worship of the universal Church, adapted
"according to the use" of a particular branch of that
Church in a particular land and country.

Today the public worship of the vast majority of Christians entails the use of such an historic liturgy. The rites of

---

[1] *Of the Laws of Ecclesiastical Polity*, V, 25, 4.

the Eastern Churches and the Roman Catholic Church are the heirs of the liturgical usages of the undivided Church of ancient times. These ancient liturgies, in turn, are directly descended from Jewish liturgies observed by our Lord and His apostles. Similarly, the prayer books of the Lutheran and Anglican Communions are not fresh inventions of the Reformation period. They are revisions of the rites of medieval, Latin Catholicism, in the light of New Testament and early Christian practices.

To a lesser degree the same traditions of worship apply to the Protestant Churches that have cultivated a more free habit of corporate prayer. The Methodists, for example, employ a liturgy based upon the English Book of Common Prayer for the administration of the sacraments. Most Presbyterian bodies have liturgical orders of worship, containing much traditional material, which are officially recommended and widely used. In our own times many of the Independent Churches, such as the Congregationalists and the Baptists, have adopted the use of service books, a thing their forefathers would have emphatically spurned. The latest addition to the ranks of historic Christian liturgies is the form of Holy Eucharist issued by the Synod of the Church of South India in January, 1950. This rite is a creative combination of the Anglican and Presbyterian traditions, with some notable borrowings from the liturgy of the Eastern Orthodox Churches.

In this chapter we shall trace briefly the story of how our liturgical heritage has come down to us. Every age has contributed its own peculiar deposit of devotion to the common whole. But there is no abrupt break in the succession. Even in times of radical revision of the heritage the basic core and shape of the Church's worship has re-

mained intact among the common possessions of the faithful people of God.

THE JEWISH BACKGROUND

The customs of worship among the Jews in the days of
our Lord were very formal and liturgical, whether in the
temple sacrifices, the Sabbath services of the synagogue,
or even in the domestic rites of the home about the family
table. It is only natural that the forms and ideas of these
Jewish liturgies, which nourished and blessed our Lord
and His first disciples, should have been carried over into
the worship of the Church. The Old Testament and its
Psalms, the festivals of Passover and Pentecost, sacred
meals, initiatory baptisms, confessions of faith in one God,
forms of thanksgiving and of benediction, and, above all,
the conception of true sacrifice as a humble and contrite
heart—all these things passed over from Judaism into
Christian worship.

The gospel records never portray our Lord actually
participating in the daily round of sacrificial offerings in
the temple. But they never suggest that He considered
them of little importance. The temple was His Father's
House, its altar was the sanctifying place of men's gifts. His
concern was not with the rules and regulations of the temple liturgy, but with the spirit and demeanor of those who
worshipped in it.[2] At one critical moment in His ministry
He cleansed the temple of unholy traffic and business in
its precincts, and with a prophet's zeal demanded that it
be a "house of prayer." Though he predicted its destruction, He did so as a judgment upon the blind disobedience
of His people to the law of righteousness.

---

[2] See especially Matt. 5:23-24.

So long as the temple stood, Christian disciples continued to resort to it for prayer, and for pilgrimage at the time of the greater festivals. Yet the temple made no direct impact upon the development of Christian worship. Nor could it have done so. For once the implications of Christian faith in our Lord's all-atoning sacrifice for sin on the Cross became clear, the offerings of the old covenant on Mount Zion were seen to be fulfilled and completed. At most the worship of the temple provided Christian faith with an insight into the meaning of sacrifice; and the language of the temple sacrifices was applied to the offering of Christ on Calvary. He was "the Lamb of God which taketh away the sin of the world."

The Jewish synagogues, on the other hand, passed on to Christianity their forms of corporate worship, having furnished the earliest converts to the Faith with their basic training in liturgical worship. The core of the synagogue service was the reading and interpretation of the Old Testament. Before and after the readings from the Law and the Prophets prayers and benedictions of praise were recited. These were not fixed in written form, but their contents were traditional, and any member of the synagogue congregation was expected to know how to pronounce them without introducing novel ideas and expressions. Also a confession of faith in one God, known as the *Shema*,[3] was recited; and probably some of the Psalms were sung. The synagogues, too, had a rite of baptism which was administered to proselytes from the Gentile world.

More important than the forms of synagogue worship

---

[3] The *Shema* consisted of Deut. 6:4-9,11:13-21, and Numbers 15:37-41. On one occasion our Lord appealed to it as the "first of all the commandments": "Hear, O Israel; the Lord our God is one Lord." (See Mark 12:29.)

was its spirit of active, corporate participation. There were no secrets or mysteries unknown to the people. Each member had his own assigned function and an opportunity to minister of his peculiar gifts, when called upon by the "ruler," or presiding officer. The gift might be of prayer or psalmody, of teaching or of prophesying, of ruling or of serving. The gifts and talents of each were ministered to the benefit of the whole.

Of far greater significance for Christian worship was our Lord's transformation of the Jewish domestic ritual of the common family meal, at the Last Supper with His disciples "in the night in which he was betrayed." [4] To the Jew every meal was a sacred act, for it was nothing less than a participation in the gifts of God's bountiful creation. Liturgical thanksgivings were offered before and after each meal by the head of the family, by means of which the food and drink were consecrated and made a means of religious communion with God and with one another. The blessing and breaking of the common loaf of bread formally opened the act of fellowship. And on special occasions, at the conclusion of the meal, a cup of wine mingled with water was solemnly blessed by the head of the company and passed around the table for each one to partake of it. The thanksgiving over the cup followed a traditional pattern: 1) Praise was offered to God for His provident care and nourishment; 2) His redemptive action in history for His people was recalled; and 3) prayer was made for the coming of His Kingdom. Our Lord took this familiar ritual and gave it a new and unforgettable interpretation, by the words He said when He distributed the bread and the cup. So the Jewish domestic liturgy became the distinc-

---

[4] See *The Holy Scriptures,* pp. 143-44.

tive liturgy of "the household of faith" (Gal. 6:10), of those who believe in Him and share the benefits of His redeeming sacrifice.

THE EARLY CHURCH

The New Testament gives us various glimpses of the earliest Christian disciples at their common prayers, when they gathered in the homes of members to break bread and celebrate with thanksgiving the wondrous grace new-found in Christ.[5] Much of their worship was informal and spontaneous, immediately inspired and led by the Spirit at work in their midst. Each one, according to his spiritual gifts, contributed to the common assembly some psalm or prayer, an exhortation or a teaching. There were times when the exuberance of the occasion led to disorder and confusion, with several trying to speak at once. But such disorder, which we know about chiefly from the church in Corinth, was strongly denounced by the apostle, who insisted that "all things be done decently and in order."

But the Christians of apostolic times were not entirely lacking in fixed elements and forms in their worship. They had taken over from the synagogue the regular reading of the Old Testament and some of its familiar prayers and hymns. There are echoes of this more formal type of praise in the great anthems that we find scattered through the pages of the Book of Revelation.[6] The prayers of the Eucharist, said over the bread and the cup, were certainly based upon the Jewish forms used by our Lord, and probably from the earliest days of the Church these thanksgiv-

---

[5] *Ibid.*, pp. 163-66.
[6] The Epistle for All Saints' Day contains some of these; Prayer Book, pp. 256-57.

ings included a recalling of the Lord's institution of the rite at the Last Supper. Formulas for use at Baptism also became fixed at a very early date, including brief questions and answers to be recited immediately before the baptismal act.[7] Then, too, we know that the Lord's Prayer was used liturgically. For the form of it contained in St. Matthew's gospel concludes the prayer with a typical Jewish doxology: "For thine is the kingdom, and the power, and the glory, for ever." This addition of the early Church is lacking in St. Luke's version of the prayer (11:2-4).

We know very little about the development of the Church's worship in the generation following the death of the original apostles and leaders. By the middle of the second century, however, we are sufficiently informed about the pattern of the liturgy generally followed in all the churches. The Sunday service was held about daybreak in some private house, where a suitable room was fitted for the common gathering. The bishop was customarily the celebrant, but in his absence a presbyter might act as his deputy. There were no furnishings in the room except the holy Table and, behind it, a few seats for the officiating clergy. Each member brought to the service his or her own offering of bread and wine, to be gathered together at the appropriate time for consecration. Deacons were posted near the Table to assist the celebrant in his ministrations, or near the door to keep watch lest any unauthorized intruder enter to molest the group.

We possess a brief description of the Sunday service from an *Apology* for Christianity written about the year 150 by a teacher in the church at Rome named Justin. A native of Samaria in Palestine, Justin was converted to

---

[7] For example, see Acts 8:36-37.

Christianity in Ephesus, and later came to Rome, where he was martyred about the year 165. He was thus well acquainted with the customs of the Church in both the East and the West. His description of the Sunday liturgy of the Church was designed to allay some scandalous gossip about its character that circulated among the pagans. For us it is invaluable testimony to the ancient shape or "order" of the Eucharist, which underlies all the later historic rites of Christendom. He says:

On Sunday we all have an assembly at the same place in the cities or countryside, and the memoirs of the apostles and the writings of the prophets are read as long as time allows. When the reader has finished the president makes an address, an admonition and an exhortation about the imitation of these good things. Then all arise together and offer prayers; and . . . when we have finished there is brought up bread and wine and water, and the president offers in like manner prayers and thanksgivings, as much as he is able, and the people cry out saying the *Amen*.

The distribution and sharing is made to each from the things over which thanks have been said, and is sent to those not present through the deacons. The well-to-do and those who are willing give according to their pleasure, each one of his own as he wishes, and what is collected is handed over to the president, and he helps widows and orphans, and those who are needy because of sickness or for any other reason, and those who are in prison and the strangers on their journeys. In short, he is a guardian to all those who are in want.[8]

Justin does not mention any singing. But we know from other sources that psalms were chanted between the lessons of Scripture. Note especially that the celebrant is allowed to say the thanksgiving over the bread and wine accord-

[8] *Apology*, I, 67.

ing to his ability. In another passage, however, Justin tells us that the content of this prayer followed a traditional pattern. The "president," he says, "offers praise and glory to the Father of all through the Name of the Son and the Holy Spirit, and gives thanks at great length because we have been counted worthy to receive these gifts from Him." [9]

A half century after Justin's time another leader in the church at Rome, a presbyter named Hippolytus, described in a brief manual called *The Apostolic Tradition* the customs and usages of the Church. What he tells us about the Eucharist, including the forms of prayer which he sets forth as a model, confirms the information that we have from Justin. Hippolytus also describes in some detail the rite of initiation into the Church which took place on Easter Even.

After the Scripture readings and their exposition were finished the candidates repaired to the font. When the water in the font had been blessed, they took off their clothes and recited to the officiating presbyter their renunciation of Satan, his pomps and his works. Then, descending into the font, they made a profession of their faith in a form closely resembling our Apostles' Creed:

"Dost thou believe in God the Father Almighty?"

"I believe."

"Dost thou believe in Christ Jesus, the Son of God,
Who was born of Holy Spirit and the Virgin Mary,
Who was crucified in the days of Pontius Pilate,
And died, and was buried,
And rose the third day living from the dead,

---

[9] *Apology,* I, 66.

And ascended into heaven,
And sat down at the right hand of the Father,
And will come to judge the living and the dead?"

"I believe."

"Dost thou believe in Holy Spirit in the Holy Church,
And the resurrection of the flesh?"

"I believe."

After each response, "I believe," the candidates were baptized. And when they had put on their clothes they were brought before the bishop in the presence of the congregation.

The bishop laid his hand upon each one severally and offered this prayer:

O Lord God, who hast vouchsafed these thy servants to be deserving of the forgiveness of sins through the washing of regeneration, and the Holy Spirit, send upon them thy grace, that they may serve thee according to thy will, for to thee is the glory, to the Father and to the Son with the Holy Spirit in the holy Church, both now and ever, world without end. Amen.

When the bishop had anointed and sealed each one on the forehead with consecrated oil, he gave them the Kiss of Peace. The Eucharist followed immediately, beginning at the Offertory, and the newly initiated participated for the first time in its holy mysteries.

To one familiar with the Prayer Book services it is easy to recognize in Hippolytus' manual the ancient form of many of their prayers and ceremonies. The prayer of the bishop at the laying on of hands, for example, is obviously the original of the similar prayer in the Prayer Book confirmation rite (p. 297). For Hippolytus' work had a wide circulation and influence throughout the ancient Church, both in the East and in the West. Most of the historic rites of Christendom are a development and expansion of his celebrated "apostolic tradition" of worship.

DEVELOPMENT OF THE HISTORIC LITURGIES

After Constantine freed the Church from the menace of persecution, in the early years of the fourth century, the Church's worship took on a new splendor and enrichment. Magnificent church buildings were erected, richly ornamented with mosaic and marble. Ceremonial was elaborated, and ritual forms took on a more stately style of rhetoric. The calendar of holy days was greatly extended, both in the anniversary commemorations of saints and martyrs and in new feasts in honor of our Lord and of His mother.

The liturgies of the churches also began to be crystallized in fixed and invariable words. One of the chief reasons for this consolidation was the desire to protect the Church from heresy. The fourth and fifth centuries were a time of great controversy in the Church over its two fundamental dogmas, the Trinity and the Incarnation.[10] By fixing the texts of the liturgies the Church protected the laity from novel and strange doctrines, which the older liberty given to celebrants in their prayers made possible. The principal churches or sees took the lead in this process and produced liturgies bearing the names of apostles or of noted defenders of the faith.

By the middle of the fifth century the chief liturgies of

---

[10] See *Chapters in Church History*, pp. 33-38; and *The Faith of the Church*, p. 14.

the Eastern Churches, those which still survive in use today, had reached virtually their final stage of development. The church in Jerusalem named its liturgy after St. James, the brother of the Lord and first "bishop" of the see.[11] The liturgy of Egypt, formed at Alexandria, was named after the traditional founder of the church there, the evangelist St. Mark. The liturgical traditions of the church in Antioch were taken over and developed at Constantinople, and produced the two liturgies named for St. Basil and St. Chrysostom, respectively.[12] In East Syria, the church of Edessa framed the liturgy of SS. Addai and Mari, named for the missionary founders of this see. This liturgy is still in use among the Nestorian Christians.

The liturgies of the church in Constantinople were carried by Orthodox missionaries to Russia and the Balkan countries, and in course of time they tended to supplant all other liturgies in use among the Orthodox Christians. There is a quality of unearthly glory about these liturgies that never fails to impress deeply all who enter sympathetically into their celebration. It has been best described in the words of a Russian embassy sent to Constantinople in the year 987 by Prince Vladimir of Kiev, to inquire about the Christian faith:

The Greeks led us to the edifices where they worship their God, and we knew not whether we were in heaven or on earth. For on earth there is no such splendor or such beauty, and we are at a loss how to describe it. We only know that God dwells

---

[11] The hymn "Let all mortal flesh keep silence" (Hymnal, 1940, No. 197) is taken from this liturgy.

[12] The Prayer of St. Chrysostom (Prayer Book, pp. 20, 34) is from the liturgy of St. Chrysostom.

there among men, and their service is fairer than the ceremonies of other nations. For we cannot forget that beauty.[13]

The spirit of Orthodox worship is marked by an awesome sense of the majesty of God, but an approach to Him that is childlike in wonder, simplicity and trust. Above all it has a profound sense of the communion of saints and the presence of the living, risen Lord.

The fixation of the liturgy in the Western churches extended over a longer period of time than it did in the East. The political and social chaos in Western Europe created by the migration and settlement of the Germanic barbarians in the fifth, sixth and seventh centuries prevented a smooth progress in consolidating the Church's rites. By the time of Pope Gregory the Great (590-604), however, the church in Rome had achieved a definitive settlement of its worship. The ritual of the Gregorian Sacramentary, and with it the marvelous corpus of plainchant, known as the Gregorian Chant, is the basis of the modern service books of the Roman Church. In its style the Roman liturgy is concise and austere. Composed at a time of "plague, pestilence, and famine, battle and murder, and sudden death," it is deeply conscious of the adversities and tribulations of the world and of man's helplessness without the defense of God and of His saints. At the center of its devotion is the sacrifice of our Lord upon the Cross for man's redemption, and it pleads for the benefits of His Passion with unadorned directness and intensity.

Almost contemporary with the organization of the Roman liturgy was the liturgy named for St. Ambrose (d.

---

[13] S. H. Cross, *The Russian Primary Chronicle,* Cambridge: Harvard University Press, 1930, p. 199.

397), which is still used in the diocese of Milan. By the middle of the seventh century the Church in Spain had completed its liturgical work in the so-called Mozarabic rite. It is still used in a few churches and chapels in Toledo and Salamanca. In Gaul (modern France) the liturgies of the various churches never achieved a final fixation or uniform observance; for the marked decline of culture and constant political unrest had a demoralizing effect upon them. The Celtic Christians in the British Isles, if we may judge from the scanty remains that have survived the destruction of time, used liturgies similar to those of Gaul, though they admitted some borrowings from Roman and Eastern sources. All of these "Gallican" liturgies passed out of use in the ninth century as a result of a liturgical reform sponsored by Charlemagne, who introduced the Roman rite throughout his dominions. Hence, with but few exceptions, the Roman liturgy became the universal tradition of worship in Western Christendom throughout the Middle Ages.

The Roman liturgy was brought to England by the missionary-monks sent thither for the conversion of the Anglo-Saxons by Pope Gregory the Great. The Venerable Bede has left us a memorable picture of the entrance of these monks into Canterbury on the Rogation Days before the feast of the Ascension in the year 597—"bearing a silver cross for their banner, and the image of our Lord and Saviour painted on a board, and singing the litany"—

We beseech thee, O Lord, in all thy mercy, that thine anger and wrath be turned away from this city, and from thy holy house, because we have sinned. Alleluia.[14]

---

[14] Bede, *Ecclesiastical History of the English Nation*, I, 25.

Church synods in England repeatedly enjoined the use of the Roman service books, holy days, and "manner of singing" the psalms and chants. It is significant that, when Charlemagne reformed the worship of the Church in Gaul by introducing the Roman rite, he entrusted the supervision of this work to an Englishman, Alcuin of York. The missal of the Roman Church today is substantially the same book that Alcuin drew up for Charlemagne on the basis of Pope Gregory's Sacramentary.

In addition to the sacramental rites of the Church there had developed by this time an elaborate system of daily liturgical devotion known as the divine office or the canonical hours. These services made up what was later to be included in the breviary, and they are the direct ancestors of the daily offices of Morning and Evening Prayer in the Prayer Book. All the clergy were supposed to recite these offices regularly, and, where possible, to chant them in the choirs of cathedrals and larger churches where several clerics usually resided.

It was the monks, however, who devoted themselves especially to the cultivation of the canonical hours. For the peculiar vocation of the monastic life is one of prayer. From the earliest times Christians had formed habits of daily personal devotions, consisting of Bible reading and prayer. But with the rise of the monastic movement in the fourth century these traditions of private devotion were developed into liturgical offices with a regular scheme for the singing of the Psalms and the reading of the Scriptures. A verse of Psalm 119, "Seven times a day do I praise thee," suggested a sevenfold division of these corporate devotions. Already in the monastic rules of St. Basil (d. 379) the canonical hours are outlined. Actually, there are eight of them: Nocturns (or Matins), Lauds, Prime, Terce, Sext, Nones, Vespers, and Compline. These hours were incorporated into the rule of St. Benedict of Nursia (d. about 547) and thus became an integral part of daily monastic life in the Western Church.

MEDIEVAL WORSHIP

The worship of the medieval Church has been the object of much unfair criticism, on the one hand, and of unduly romantic enthusiasm on the other. Perhaps the most notable fact about it was that the services were conducted in a language not understood by the people, but only by those with a Latin education—for the most part, the clergy and the monks. Yet there were many of the parish clergy who had a very faulty knowledge of Latin, so that they could not even pronounce the ritual accurately. In a letter of Pope Zacharias to St. Boniface we are told of a Bavarian priest who was so ignorant that he baptized "in the Name of the Fatherland *(patria)* and the Daughter *(filia)* and the Holy Spirit." [15] Similar examples could doubtless be multiplied.

The preservation of the liturgy in Latin probably operated in the long run to the benefit of the Church. It saved both the integrity and the intelligibility of worship for the day when it could be safely translated into the vernacular. The languages of modern Europe evolved through long stages, and for centuries the differences of dialect, even from village to village, were marked. Latin gave a sense of unity to the Church's worship that it could not otherwise have had. It made it possible for Christians of differing

---

[15] *The Letters of Saint Boniface,* translated with an introduction by Ephraim Emerton; New York: Columbia University Press, 1940, pp. 122-23.

hearths and homes to join in a common rite. Moreover, books were scarce and expensive, since they had to be copied by hand. Until the invention of printing (15th century) there was no possibility of placing in the hands of all the people the service books of the Church. Even most parish clergy could not afford to own a Bible; and such knowledge of the Scriptures as they had was derived from the lessons written out in the service books. Their capacity for teaching was dependent upon what opportunities of education they themselves had enjoyed, and this was often little enough. Only a fortunate few had any kind of theological education.

It was inevitable that, given this cultural situation, the worship of the Church should be subject to considerable abuse; for superstition is the child of ignorance. All too often the rites of the Church were expected to operate like a charm, and their graces sought as if they were some miraculous magic. The supernatural world was very close to the medieval mind. The saints were constantly invoked to ward off the Devil and his imps. But it is possible to exaggerate the superstitious elements in medieval religion, and forget that its rites also produced in countless thousands of all classes of society "the spirit of true godliness and holy fear." A ritual that could inspire men to build the great cathedrals that enshrined it, to adorn it with exquisite taste and beauty, and above all, to love charity as the mother of all virtues, was not dead though it were celebrated in an unknown tongue.

The most serious consequence of the use of Latin was that it gave the clergy a kind of monopoly over the liturgy. The people ceased to be active participants and became spectators in worship. The sanctuary was a stage for a mystery drama which they watched, whose benefits they received, but to which they contributed little except the necessary fees and tithes and bequests to keep it going. Their offerings ceased to be an integral part of the eucharistic action. They seldom communicated more than once a year, at Easter. But they paid for what they received.

Indeed the money transactions associated with the saying of masses developed into a serious abuse. A wealthy rake could believe his salvation was secure by leaving a large sum, the income of which could support a priest to do nothing but say mass for the repose of his soul. The Church, of course, never really taught that a man could buy his way into heaven. But in the popular mind escape from Purgatory was a long and expensive path. The tragedy of this situation lay in the degradation of the whole concept of the priesthood, when it could be used for this kind of traffic in the sacrament.

Because the liturgy was a monopoly of specialists, it tended to become overly elaborate. It is tedious to repeat the same formularies over and over again day after day. Hence there developed all sorts of variation in the liturgy by way of elaborating "proper" texts that changed with each new holy day. By the later centuries of the Middle Ages there was hardly a day that was not dedicated to the memory of some saint. And each new day had its own set of proper liturgical texts.

A great number of liturgical books had to be coordinated for the full celebration of the ritual. One contained the chants, another the lessons, another the prayers, and so on. One book included all the rules—what was to be read, when it should come in the service, and how it was to be rendered. This book was popularly called in England the Pie. Cranmer's remark about it in the preface of the first Prayer Book of 1549 is justly famous:

Moreover, the number and hardness of the rules called the Pie, and the manifold changings of the service, was the cause, that to turn the book only, was so hard and intricate a matter, that many times, there was more business to find out what should be read, than to read it when it was found out.

When a liturgy has become so complicated that only experts can manage it, and the laity have no effective participation in it, it comes very close to ceasing to be a "liturgy" at all.[16]

Though the Roman liturgy served as the common core of the medieval Church's worship, there was no such thing as a uniform observance of it. Every diocese and monastic order had its own adaptations and variations of it—what we call "uses." Bishops exercised a great deal of freedom in supplementing or altering the Roman usages. England was no exception to this custom. In the later Middle Ages many English dioceses, including Canterbury, adopted the "Use" of the see of Sarum, now known as Salisbury. At the time of the Reformation, Archbishop Cranmer adopted the Sarum service books as the basis for his work of revision and reform; but for some details he borrowed forms from other diocesan uses. For example, some of the phrases in the marriage service—the charge to the couple, and the giving away of the bride—come from the Use of York. Only after the invention of printing could any kind of uniformity be established or enforced.

The continual round of religious services day after day in all the churches and monasteries was a conspicuous fea-

---

[16] See Chapter III, pp. 51 ff.

ture of medieval life. Though much of it was conventional and routine, it had a deeper significance. A modern scholar who is not unaware of the liturgical "decay" of the medieval Church, has said of it on the more positive side that

. . . religion did penetrate all human life then with a hopefulness and a purpose beyond its human littleness which it is very hard to imagine in our secularized society. That continual solemn and public rendering of society's worship and thanksgiving for redemption in the choirs of Christendom by day and night did keep the fact of redemption before men's thoughts continually. Any setting aside and maintenance of large delegations of men for the *business* of public worship, to *do* it on behalf of their fellows continually . . . does in itself glorify God and edify men and sanctify life, because it publicly acknowledges in the most obvious way the claim of the spirit over the body and of God over all the temporal living of men.[17]

THE REFORMATION OF THE LITURGY

Reform of the Church's worship was one aspect of that larger Reformation movement of the sixteenth century in Christian doctrine, morals and organization.[18] Nor was concern with the liturgy confined to the Protestant reformers. The Roman Catholic Church also produced a thorough-going revision of its inherited rites in the same century. All of these reforms, whether Catholic or Protestant, reacted one upon another. It is commonly conceded that the work of liturgical reform accomplished in England exhibited unusual marks of genius. For this we are chiefly

[17] G. Dix, *The Shape of the Liturgy*, London: Dacre Press [A. & C. Black], 1945, p. 604.
[18] See *Chapters in Church History*, pp. 133 ff.

indebted to the learning and literary skill of Thomas Cranmer, Archbishop of Canterbury from 1533 to 1556. The two Prayer Books issued in the reign of Edward VI, the first in 1549, the second in 1552, are in large measure his work.

The basis of Cranmer's reform, as already noted, was the Sarum adaptation of the Roman liturgy. He also made large use, especially in the revision of the Divine Office, of a reformed Breviary issued by the Spanish Cardinal Quiñones, a work originally commissioned by the Pope. Cranmer was personally acquainted with Lutheran experiments in liturgical reform, and borrowed freely from them, notably from a liturgy set forth by Archbishop Hermann of Cologne, a prelate of Lutheran sympathies. The Greek liturgies of St. Basil and St. Chrysostom were likewise used by Cranmer, and he knew some of the old Gallican liturgies. From all these sources Cranmer derived ideas, forms and phrases. Thus the whole heritage of the Church's worship contributed to the making of the Book of Common Prayer.

The principles guiding Cranmer and his associates in their work were these. 1) The liturgical offices were to be simplified by eliminating many variable elements. They were shortened in length. And, of course, they were put into English. Thus the common prayer of the Church was to be easily manageable and readily understood by all the people, clergy and laity, learned and unlearned. The rites of the Church were so simplified that they could all be included in the covers of one book; and this book, with the Bible, would furnish all that was necessary for the celebration of the liturgy. Incidentally, this was a great saving in cost, and furthermore it meant that the entire liturgy of the Church could ultimately be placed in the hands of all the people.

2) The liturgy was revised on the basis of the Holy Scriptures. The doctrine of the Prayer Book was to conform to Biblical teaching. Legendary and "uncertain" materials which had found their way into the ritual texts, especially in the observance of saint's days, were eliminated. There "is ordained nothing to be read," said Cranmer, "but the very pure word of God, the holy scriptures, or that which is evidently grounded upon the same." This principle of conformity to Scripture was not narrowly applied, however. The English Reformers did not follow the principle of Calvin, that the Church's worship should include only what was specifically enjoined in Scripture. They followed the broader view of Luther that all things that were edifying in the older forms and manner of worship should be kept, except what was definitely contrary to Scripture.

The liturgy of the first Prayer Book of 1549 was therefore conservative in its character. The form and structure of the old rites remained the same. Most of the old ceremonies and ornaments were kept. The people could recognize a real continuity in their customs of worship. There were some radical features. The old system of eight canonical hours was reduced to two: the orders for Morning and Evening Prayer. But with the dissolution of the monasteries there was no need for the lengthier and more elaborate daily offices. The two offices were practically suited to the needs and opportunities of both the parish clergy and the lay people. More serious was the elimination from the calendar of holy days of all feasts and anniversaries of saints other than those suggested by the New Testament.

This was indeed a great loss in the people's remembrance of the wealth of the communion of saints. Yet it was recognized on all sides that some reform was necessary in the calendar. It had become overloaded and top-heavy.

In many instances great gains were made in restoring the liturgical rites of the Church to a pattern more nearly like those of the early Church. The Holy Communion became a corporate act again, including regular offerings by the people both of alms for the poor and of the oblations of bread and wine. Non-communicating attendance at the service was discouraged. The burial offices were purged of the gloomy foreboding of Purgatory, as then understood, and given the note of resurrection joy and triumph so characteristic of the early Church's rites for the departed. Confirmation was restored to its ancient significance as a completion of Christian initiation and a requirement for admission to full communicant status.

It was inevitable that the strenuous controversies of the Reformation era should leave their mark upon the reform of the liturgy. Those of strongly Protestant sympathies felt that the first Prayer Book of 1549 had not gone far enough in reaction against certain medieval abuses. Any suggestion that the Eucharist was a propitiatory sacrifice for sin, and any trace of the dogma of transubstantiation, as a definition of the Real Presence of our Lord in the sacrament, were especially abhorrent to them. Hence when these men gained the ascendency in the later years of Edward VI's reign, they issued a revision of the Prayer Book in 1552 more agreeable to their views. In this Book the Holy Communion rite was very much rearranged. All mention of the Offertory of bread and wine was eliminated; and the Consecration Prayer was broken into several parts, some of them placed before, and some after, communion. At the communion, instead of the formula "The Body of our Lord Jesus Christ," etc., there was substituted the phrase "Take and eat this in remembrance," etc.

At the last minute, shortly before the Book was issued for use, a rubric was inserted, solely on the authority of the King's Council and over the protest of Archbishop Cranmer, which declared that by kneeling to receive the sacrament was not meant

. . . that any adoration is done, or ought to be done, either unto the Sacramental bread or wine there bodily received, or unto any real and essential presence there being of Christ's natural flesh and blood.

This is the famous Black Rubric, so named from the bold-faced black type with which it was printed.

The second Prayer Book was short-lived in England. Eight months after its issuance King Edward was dead, and the Catholic reaction under Queen Mary swept away almost the whole work of reform by the restoration of the old Latin rites. Queen Elizabeth, however, restored the use of the second Prayer Book in 1559, but with several important revisions. In particular, the doctrine of our Lord's Real Presence in the Eucharist was safeguarded, by combining the Words of Administration of both the 1549 and the 1552 Books (see Prayer Book, pp. 82-83). The Black Rubric was eliminated. Her policy was one of conciliation toward moderate men of both Catholic and Protestant persuasion.[19] In this she was eminently successful, and the settlement of religion in her reign has substantially endured until the present day. Some additions were made to the Prayer Book

---

[19] See *Chapters in Church History*, pp. 174-75.

in 1604 in the reign of James I. After the Puritan Common-wealth had proscribed the use of the Prayer Book for fifteen years, a general revision of the liturgy was accomplished in 1661 with the restoration of the monarchy under Charles II. But the liturgy of the Church of England today is basically the same as it was when established in the Elizabethan era.

THE PRAYER BOOK IN AMERICA

The English liturgy accompanied the first permanent settlers in America, and was in use in all Anglican churches in the colonies until the American Revolution. We have a vivid description of the first services at Jamestown, Virginia, from the pen of Captain John Smith:

When I first went to Virginia, I well remember, wee did hang an awning (which is an old saile) to three or four trees to shadow us from the Sunne, our walls were rales of wood, our seats unhewed trees, till we cut plankes; our Pulpit a bar of wood nailed to two neighboring trees; in foule weather we shifted into an old rotten tent, for wee had few better, and this came by the way of adventure for new. This was our Church, till wee built a homely thing like a barne, set upon cratchets, covered with rafts, sedge, and earth; so was also the walls; the best of our houses of the like curiosity, but the most parte farre much worse workmanship, that could neither well defend wind nor raine, yet wee had daily Common Prayer morning and evening, every Sunday two Sermons, and every three months the holy Communion, till our Minister died. But our Prayers daily, with an Homily on Sundaies, we continued two or three yeares after, till more Preachers came.[20]

Under these conditions the first service of Holy Com-

---

[20] Quoted in W. S. Perry, *The History of the American Episcopal Church,* 1587-1883, Vol. I, Boston: James R. Osgood and Co., 1885, pp. 45-46.

munion was celebrated by the chaplain of the colony, the Rev. Robert Hunt, on June 21, 1607, the Third Sunday after Trinity.

The severing of political ties with England resulting from the American Revolution necessarily involved the independent organization of the Episcopal Church in the United States. For in England the King is the temporal head of the Church. Thus alterations in the prayers for civil rulers had to be made in the American Prayer Book. At the first General Convention, held in Philadelphia in 1789, these changes were duly made, and the Convention took advantage of "the happy occasion, which was offered to them . . . to take a further review of the Public Service, and to establish such other alterations and amendments therein as might be deemed expedient." But care was taken to maintain the principle that "this Church is far from intending to depart from the Church of England in any essential point of doctrine, discipline, or worship; or further than local circumstances require." [21]

One very important change in the liturgy was made, however. In place of the Consecration Prayer of the Holy Communion in the English Prayer Book, the Convention adopted the form of consecration in the Scottish Prayer Book of 1764. The efforts of Bishop Samuel Seabury of Connecticut brought this to pass. Bishop Seabury had been consecrated by the Bishops of the Episcopal Church in Scotland.[22] With them he had drawn up a concordat in which he promised, among other things, to introduce the Scottish communion service in his own diocese, and also,

---

[21] From the Preface of the Prayer Book, p. vi.
[22] See *Chapters in Church History*, pp. 220-221, 224-225.

if possible, in the Episcopal Church in America whenever it should be organized on a national basis.

The Scottish form for the Holy Communion is much closer to the model of the 1549 Prayer Book than the English. But the learned bishops of the Scottish Church were also keen students of the ancient liturgies of the Church, especially those of the Eastern Orthodox Churches. Their Consecration Prayer was a creative combination of the 1549 rite with material derived from the Eastern liturgies. Thus the Holy Communion in the American Prayer Book has a rich and varied ancestry. It derives through both the English and Scottish branches of Anglicanism from the ancient traditions of worship of both the Greek and the Latin Churches.

The American Prayer Book has undergone two extensive revisions since 1789. The first one, completed in 1892, marked the centennial of our Church's independent life in the nation. It was promoted by a strong desire to make the liturgy more adaptable to the needs of our varied American life and culture. The Prayer Book was much enriched by new material drawn from both ancient and modern sources. The second revision, which culminated in 1928, carried these aims of enrichment and adaptability even further. There are few liturgies in use in any Church today that can equal the American Prayer Book for its remarkable combination of loyalty to tradition and breadth of material. There are deposited in its pages the devotions of all ages of Christian faith and piety. Some of these prayers are as old as Christianity itself. There are others that have been composed by persons still living among us.

Throughout the world today the Anglican Communion

is spread abroad in more than 300 dioceses, and counts some forty million members. This great fellowship of Christians is bound together in unity by a common faith and a common worship. More than anything else the Prayer Book is the basis of this communion. It is not exactly the same Book everywhere. Not only the English, the Scottish and the American Churches have their own adaptations of a common tradition, but the Churches in Ireland, Canada, and South Africa have their respective variations of it. Similarly, in the Churches in China, India, the West Indies, and in single missionary dioceses scattered afar, local and provincial rites are being developed out of the mother liturgy.

The worship of Anglicans is always in the language of the people. For it is fundamental to our tradition that common prayer must be corporate and "understanded of the people." To this end the Prayer Book has been translated into all the principal tongues and dialects of all the continents and isles. The present Archbishop of Canterbury has recently written:

Wherever we go throughout our Communion we find ourselves at home in a worship scriptural, catholic, congregational, understanded of the people, simple and profound, of which the standard and exemplar is the Book of Common Prayer. That knits us together indeed. That lies at the root of our fellowship with one another. And it is deeply moving to know that the older and the younger churches of our Communion alike find in this tradition the same values of catholic truth, scriptural soundness and evangelical zeal.[23]

[23] "The Mission of the Anglican Communion," *Pan-Anglican*, Vol. I, No. 1 (Lent, 1950), p. 5.

PART II

The Book of Common Prayer

CHAPTER FIVE

The Christian Year

IT COMES as a surprise to many people, upon opening the Book of Common Prayer for the first time, to discover that it begins with an almanac. The introductory portion contains some fifty pages filled with calendar notes, time tables and schedules. Again, in the very heart of the Book, almost one-third of its contents are given over to specific prayers and lessons assigned to every Sunday and other stated days of the year. Closer scrutiny of the Prayer Book will reveal that its entire contents are laid out according to an ordered time-sequence of rites and observances.

The initial services in the Book provide our corporate morning and evening devotions, day by day, year in and year out. Each service, every day, has its own appointed psalms and Bible lessons, as set forth in the tables of the introduction. In addition, a series of occasional Prayers and Thanksgivings, the Litany, and A Penitential Office, present us with appropriate forms for various and special occasions and needs that recur from time to time in the daily round of our common life as Churchmen and as citizens.

The middle section of the Prayer Book—the heart of its contents—includes the Order for the Holy Communion, with the Collects, Epistles and Gospels for the specified

Sundays and Holy Days. There is no rule, of course, that limits the celebration of Holy Communion to these days. In many places it is celebrated daily. When our Lord instituted the sacrament and commanded His disciples to repeat it in thankful remembrance of Him, He did not say how often they should observe it. Yet from its earliest days the Church has deemed it fitting to celebrate the Holy Communion on Sundays and other festal anniversaries when faithful disciples come together for their corporate worship. Thus week by week and year by year the Body of His faithful servants throughout the world and throughout all generations has been sustained and nourished by continual communion in Him.

There follows a third section in the Prayer Book, containing Occasional Offices that mark successive stages of our growth in life's ongoing way from birth to death. The spiritual rebirth of Baptism follows upon our natural birth in time. Confirmation comes at the maturing time, when we reach years of discretion and personal responsibility. Then at the momentous decisions and crises of marriage, childbirth, sickness and death, the liturgy seals the event with the blessing of God. It relates these significant times to His ultimate redeeming and sanctifying purposes, both for our own selves and for the living fellowship of all His people.

The liturgy of the Church takes time seriously. Just as our ordinary daily tasks and activities are regulated by clocks and calendars, so also our spiritual life and growth are ordered by "times and seasons." By means of the prayers and praises of the daily offices, the recurring cycle of the Christian Year, and the occasional rites of dedication and of blessing, the liturgy helps us to "redeem the time." And the things that are temporal become sacraments of the things that are eternal.

CHRISTIANITY AND TIME

The liturgy takes time seriously because the Christian faith takes time seriously. Philosophers may tell us that time is only an illusion, a glimpse of that eternity which God alone knows as an everlasting present. The scientist may define it as man's device to measure the repeated courses of the heavenly bodies or of the heart's beat. Yet no definition can enable us to escape it. For time is an inevitable condition of our creatureliness. It is part of the givenness of our human existence. God has set us within the mysterious ordering of time that we may grow with it in His grace and spend it to His glory.

God's gift of time is a priceless possession. Time that is lost or wasted or misused can never be recovered. A misspent past can only be redeemed by repentance and a resolute change of our wills and affections. God's forgiveness of our past wrongs wipes out the shame and the guilt. But the painful consequences of sin are not easily effaced or overcome. Dreadful as it is, the truth is inescapable that "the iniquity of the fathers" is visited "upon the children and upon the children's children." The evil effects of war and human slavery are the most obvious illustrations of this judgment of God upon our sins. From this judgment the opening cry of the Litany derives its poignant relevance:

Remember not, Lord, our offenses, nor the offenses of our forefathers; neither take thou vengeance of our sins:

Spare us, good Lord.

Yet time need not ever be lost. It can always be improved and won. This also is part and parcel of its priceless character. Each moment of the living present is an opportunity of decision, of decision for the right, "as God gives us to see the right." Such decisions have lasting consequences. Each one of them, too, opens new possibilities of choice for growth in God's love and service.

> If on our daily course our mind
> Be set to hallow all we find,
> New treasures still, of countless price,
> God will provide for sacrifice.

We miss the full force of time's opportunities of decision if we fail to realize their urgency. The time for right choices is now. Tomorrow may be, and usually is, too late.

Nothing is more characteristic of the gospel story than our Lord's insistence upon the necessity of decision *now*. "The time is fulfilled, and the kingdom of God is at hand: repent ye, and believe the gospel" (Mark 1:15). "No man, having put his hand to the plough, and looking back, is fit for the kingdom of God" (Luke 9:62). "Watch ye therefore: for ye know not when the master of the house cometh . . . lest coming suddenly he find you sleeping" (Mark 13:35-36). In these three sayings our Lord demands that we seize the present moment for decision, neither looking back for fond memories of the past, nor unready for the crises that the future brings.

Because our decisions in the here and now have a lasting consequence, the drama of history has meaning. Each single event of history has a unique, once-for-all significance. The causes, circumstances and effects of the events of history may have many similarities, but they are never exactly the same. So also are the persons who play their respective roles in these events. They are never types but always individuals. History is different because this or that particular person made, or did not make, a particular decision at a particular time and place. For history is not a cycle of meaningless repetitions. It is a process and a progress of men's thoughts and deeds, for good or for ill, until the day when God shall judge them by our Lord Jesus Christ.[1]

History is also the sphere in which God reveals to men His saving purpose and His unfailing judgment. He stoops to make Himself known to us under our own conditions and limits of time and space. It was the peculiar genius of the Hebrew prophets that they saw the hand of God at work within the events of their own times, to bless and to punish, to forewarn and to overrule. One of the biting remarks our Lord made about the religious leaders of His own day concerned their inability to "discern the signs of the times." The New Testament faith, and all that follows from it, is rooted in the recognition that God acted in history uniquely in the person of Jesus Christ.

The Incarnation is not an idea or a theory but a historic event that has happened once and once only, in an individual man, subject as are all men to the limitations of time and place. Yet it was no chance happening, but one prepared by the providence of God and given at the proper, ripe time. "When the fulness of the time was come," said St. Paul, "God sent forth his Son, made of a woman" (Gal. 4:4). Nor was He made of any woman, but of a particu-

[1] See *The Faith of the Church*, pp. 106, 107.

larly chosen woman, named Mary, of the lineage of David, espoused to a man named Joseph.

The Christian religion, like its parent Judaism, is commonly described as a historic faith—not because it has a long history or because it has made history—but because its faith is grounded upon the action of God in history. The persons and events of history are of the very essence of its gospel. In the very heart of its Creed one finds a chronological reference: He was crucified under Pontius Pilate. An ordinary Roman provincial governor has thus been accorded a lasting, though unenviable, fame because of a judicial murder he permitted during his term of office in Judaea. Roman magistrates raised many crosses for the punishment of malefactors. But this one particular cross, the Cross of Jesus, God made the destroyer of death and thereby opened the Kingdom of Heaven to all believers.

THE LITURGY AND TIME

The time pattern of the liturgy continually confronts us with ever new moments of decision. This is obvious with respect to the occasional offices. Baptism is a once-for-all renunciation of evil, a profession of allegiance, and a promise of obedience. Its gift of spiritual birth can never be repeated. In Confirmation a definite acceptance of Jesus Christ as Lord and Saviour is promised. A once-for-all gift of the Spirit is imparted for our daily increase in His manifold gifts of grace. A life-long pledge of fidelity and love is exchanged by the parties to Holy Matrimony—a decision that is binding until death.

The day-to-day and week-by-week worship of the Church makes the same decisive demands upon us for response to God here and now. They are no meaningless cycle, any more than history itself, of vain repetitions. Unless we make a mockery of them our lives must of necessity be different after every act of participation in them. In the daily offices of Morning and Evening Prayer we confess our past sins and pray for God's forgiveness, "that we may *hereafter* live a godly, righteous, and sober life." And the priest, in the Absolution, exhorts us to prayer for true repentance and the gift of the Holy Spirit, "that those things may please him which we do *at this present;* and that the rest of our life *hereafter* may be pure and holy."

Similarly in the penitential portions of the Holy Communion, past, present, and future are incisively distinguished. In the Invitation we are called to repent of our sins past, to be "in love and charity with our neighbours" now, and to "intend to lead a new life" in the future. The General Confession repeats these resolves: "Forgive us all that is past; and grant that we may ever hereafter serve and please thee in newness of life." Again, the Absolution asks God to "pardon and deliver" us from all our sins past, to "confirm and strengthen [us] in all goodness" now in this present, and to bring us finally "to everlasting life."

The annually recurring seasons of the Christian Year also afford us ever new opportunities for a fresh start. This is stated with special emphasis in the Sunday Epistles read at the beginning of our preparatory seasons for the two great festivals of Christmas and Easter:

And that, knowing the time, that now it is high time to awake out of sleep: for now is our salvation nearer than when we believed. The night is far spent, the day is at hand: let us therefore cast off the works of darkness, and let us put on the armour of light. (Prayer Book, pp. 90-91.)

For he saith, I have heard thee in a time accepted, and in the day of salvation have I succoured thee: behold, now is the accepted time; behold, now is the day of salvation. (Prayer Book, p. 126.)

The late Dean William Palmer Ladd of the Berkeley Divinity School often reminded his students of the cogent force of the word *now* in our Advent Collect—this word makes vividly real to us in the present time both the first coming of our Lord in His Incarnation and His second coming in Judgment.[2] In a similar way this opening Collect of the Christian Year is matched by the Collect for St. Andrew's Day, which stands at the head of the calendar of saint's days in the Prayer Book. As the apostle "readily obeyed the calling" of Christ and "followed him without delay," so we pray that "we, being called by thy holy Word, may *forthwith* give up ourselves obediently to fulfil thy holy commandments" (Prayer Book, p. 226).

Every season and every holy day of the Christian Year is for us an advent, a coming in the present time of God's mighty acts of old in His Christ and in His saints. When we "make memorial" of them we relive them as though we ourselves were the very historic participants in the drama, the very ones who were summoned to make choice and take a stand for God and for His Christ. God's revelation of Himself, His redeeming mercies given to His people in past ages, the witness of His saints and martyrs to His truth—all these wondrous events of history are made present to us here and now, that we may appropriate them for our very own.

---

[2] Prayer Book, p. 90. See W. P. Ladd, *Prayer Book Interleaves*, New York: Oxford University Press, 1942, p. 28.

The Jewish rabbis used to say of the Passover observance that "in every generation a man must so regard himself as if he came forth himself out of Egypt." [3] The same principle holds good of our Christian Year. In Advent we look forward to the coming of Messiah in company with the prophets and heralds of the Old Testament. At Christmas we join the shepherds in worship and adoration of the new-born Babe. At Epiphany we bring to Him our treasures in company with the Magi. In the fast of Lent we join our Lord for "forty days and forty nights" in His retreat in the wilderness. Through Passiontide and Eastertide we take with Him "joyfully the sufferings of the present time, in full assurance of the glory that shall be revealed" (Prayer Book, p. 144). And at His Ascension to the Father we pray that we "may also in heart and mind thither ascend, and with him continually dwell" (Prayer Book, p. 177). Note, too, how the brief phrase "as at this time," in the Collect for Whitsunday, makes the outpouring of the Spirit on the apostles at Pentecost almost two thousand years ago an ever renewed and renewing experience of our own.[4]

We owe to the genius of the Jews this distinctive character of our sacred feasts and fasts. Originally the Hebrew people, like their pagan neighbours, built their religious observances about the seasonal courses of nature or of the heavenly bodies. But the insight of the prophets into God's workings in history led the Jewish leaders who codified the Law after the Exile to reinterpret the calendar as days of

---

[3] *The Mishnah,* translated by H. Danby, New York: Oxford University Press, 1933, p. 151.

[4] Prayer Book, p. 180. Cf. the same phrase in the Christmas Collect, p. 96.

historical commemoration. Passover, for example, was in origin a spring moon festival combined with an ingathering of the first-fruits of spring harvest. It became the celebration of the deliverance of Israel from the bondage of Egypt. Yet it was always more than a recalling of this supreme act of God's redemption of His people. The Passover was also the promise of a future deliverance from present oppressors when God should establish His Kingdom. From the moral viewpoint Passover was deliverance from the bondage of sin, by the putting away of "old leaven," the sour dough from a past baking, and the eating of unleavened bread as a sign of a new, fresh start in life wholly consecrated to God.

The link between the Jewish calendar of the Old Testament and the Christian calendar of the New Testament is that Passover celebration when Jesus of Nazareth was slain, as it were a Paschal lamb, and rose again the third day, "the firstfruits" of them that sleep in sin and death. From the beginning Christian faith has seen in this event the end of one era of history and the dawn of another. More than that, the Passion and Resurrection of Christ were the very opening of the age to come, when history itself shall have an end and God's triumph over sin and death shall be manifestly complete. The Christian Passover is the celebration of the final deliverance by God of His people, the formation of the New Israel of God, the Church, and the foretaste of His everlasting and eternal Kingdom. Thus in the Christian festival the past event is commemorated and the future consummation is anticipated. But the feast is neither mere remembrance nor unfulfilled hope. It is a present reality in the hearts of faithful believers.

THE PRIMACY OF EASTER

"If Christ be not raised," said St. Paul, "your faith is vain; ye are yet in your sins" (1 Cor. 15:17). Easter Day, both by origin and by right, is the primary festival of Christians, "the royal feast of feasts." Almost the entire Christian Year depends upon its date—hence the large place given in the Prayer Book's introductory pages to the tables for reckoning the date of Easter. Every Sunday is a commemoration of Easter, the first day of the week, when the Lord rose triumphant from the grave. Every rite of Baptism, wherein we die unto sin and arise unto righteousness, is a reminder of Easter. Every celebration of the Holy Communion recalls not only the "night in which he was betrayed" but also how the risen Lord made Himself known to His disciples in the breaking of bread. The burial office begins with our Lord's emphatic promise, "I am the resurrection and the life"; for, as the early Christians spoke of it, the physical death of a Christian is but his "birthday in eternity."

The fifty days from Easter to Pentecost was the only festival observed by the universal Church during the first three centuries of its history. The period was one continuous season of joy in the wondrous events of our redemption through our Lord's Passion, Resurrection, Ascension and Gift of the Holy Spirit. The note of joy was especially evident in the singing of Alleluia, a paean of praise adopted from the Jewish ritual of the Passover, which included the Alleluia Psalms (Nos. 113-118). These psalms, now infused with a Christian interpretation, provided the earliest hymnody of the Church. One verse of them in particular marked the psalmody chanted between the lessons at the Eucharist: "This is the day which the Lord hath made; we will rejoice and be glad in it." [5] The *day* for Christians was, of course, Easter.

Only in the fourth century was the unity of the season broken up into a series of specific commemorations: the ceremonies of the several days of Holy Week; the restriction of Easter Day and Pentecost to the memorial of the Resurrection and the Coming of the Holy Spirit, respectively; and the institution of Ascension Day forty days after Easter. This new development was the direct result of interest in the sites of Biblical story in Palestine after the peace of the Church from persecution. Both Constantine and his mother sponsored these investigations in the Holy Land, which produced such "finds" as the Mount of Calvary, the true Cross upon which the Saviour died, the Holy Sepulchre, the Garden of Gethsemane, and the exact spot on the Mount of Olives whence our Lord ascended into Heaven. Magnificent churches were erected over these hallowed places; while the church in Jerusalem promoted colorful services dramatizing the events associated with these sites. Pilgrims from all over the Christian world, impressed by these commemorations, carried home detailed descriptions of them. Before long churches all over Christendom were imitating the Jerusalem cycle of observances, from the procession of palms on the Sunday before Easter to the commemoration of the Ascension on the fortieth day after Easter.

Easter was designated as the appropriate time for initiation of new members into the fellowship of the Church. During a long vigil service on Easter Even candidates

---

[5] Psalm 118:24. Note the survival of this verse as an opening sentence at Morning Prayer on Easter Day, Prayer Book, p. 5.

were baptized and confirmed, and at dawn on Easter Day they made their first communion. Those hindered from being initiated at this time were afforded a second opportunity at the close of the season, on the eve of Pentecost. In this way the Church dramatized for the new recruits the mystery of their redemption: their death and burial with Christ unto sin, and their resurrection with Him unto newness of life in the power of His Holy Spirit.

Out of the disciplines preparatory to baptism on Easter Even there developed the season of Lent. Candidates were given an intensive instruction in Christian faith and morals, based upon the Bible and the Creed, and submitted themselves to fasting and other exercises of self-denial. At first the period of discipline was of short duration, varying anywhere from two days to a week. But by the time of the Council of Nicaea in 325 most of the churches had adopted a Lenten fast of six weeks, or roughly forty days, corresponding to our Lord's forty-day retreat in the wilderness.[6] By this time also, not only the candidates for baptism but all the faithful were enjoined to participate in the Lenten disciplines as a strengthening of their own devotion.

The Collects, Epistles and Gospels for the Lenten and Eastertide seasons still preserve many reminiscences of these ancient disciplines connected with Christian initiation. The Gospel for the First Sunday in Lent set before the candidates the Lord's own renunciation of the world, the flesh and the Devil, renunciations that they themselves would make at their baptism. Indeed, all the Lenten les-

---

[6] Since Sundays are never fast days, a six-week Lent gives only thirty-six days of fasting. At Rome, in the sixth century, an exact forty-day period was achieved by adding to the season the four days before the first Sunday in Lent, beginning Ash Wednesday.

sons were chosen for purposes of instruction. The Epistles, especially, set forth the great contrasts between heathen and Christian life: uncleanness versus holiness, darkness versus light, bondage versus freedom, dead works versus living service of God.

In the Epistle for the First Sunday after Easter there is a reference to the "three that bear witness, the Spirit, and the water, and the blood" (Prayer Book, pp. 170-71). To the newly-baptized these three witnesses were the sacramental mysteries of Baptism, Confirmation and Eucharist, which they had experienced the previous week. Throughout Eastertide the lessons continued the instruction. The Epistles teach self-control and readiness to suffer for the truth in witness to one's faith. The Gospels introduce the newly-baptized to the guiding and strengthening power of the Holy Spirit now available to them. In Whitsun Week many of the lessons treat specifically of the mysteries of baptism and confirmation and of their relation to our life in the Spirit.

During the sixth century the church in Rome set apart the three Sundays before Lent as days of special supplication for God's help and protection against the ravages of war, plague and famine. Because of their penitential character they serve as a kind of pre-Lenten preparation, if not an actual extension of the Lenten discipline itself. About the same time the older custom of preparing candidates for baptism during Lent began to fall into disuse. The result was a shift in emphasis in the Church's teaching about Lenten observance. The stress was now put upon penitence. Yet the older idea of Lent as a time of disciplined preparation for Easter was never entirely lost. In our own day we are recovering again the positive values of Lent as an opportunity for the deepening and strengthening of our knowledge and devotion. Certainly a Lenten observance that does not make us better-informed, better-disciplined Christians come Easter-time has missed the fundamental purpose of the season.

SUNDAY

Each Sunday of the year is a reminder of Easter Day. Already in New Testament times Sunday was known as the Lord's Day.[7] There is no more telling indication of the primacy of the Easter faith among Christians than the way Sunday supplanted the Jewish Sabbath as the day above all days for the worship of God. The holiness of the Sabbath was one of the most inviolable laws of God revealed in the Old Testament. Nothing in our Lord's teaching or practice suggested that He considered the Sabbath of little importance. He made it clear, however, that He held the Sabbath rest to be sacred, not in the negative sense of refraining from all labor, but in the positive opportunity it afforded both for worship and for loving service to those in need. The Jewish disciples of our Lord continued to observe the Sabbath so long as they lived. There is no hint in the New Testament of any disfavor expressed towards those Christians who continued to keep the Sabbath law.

The transfer from Sabbath to Sunday in Christian usage was more by way of accident than design. But once it had taken place the Church saw in the change the working of the Spirit in a new age in the history of the people of God. As Canon Liddon put it, "The Lord's Day marks the completed Redemption, as the Sabbath had marked the com-

---

[7] Rev. 1:10. Note the collect for "Sunday Morning," Prayer Book, p. 595.

pleted Creation." The Resurrection of Jesus Christ "on the first day of the week" is the most stupendous event in the history of mankind, from the day of man's creation until God's final judgment at the end of time. Sunday is our continual reminder of this basic faith and hope. It is, in the words of the poet Henry Vaughan,

> A taste of Heav'n on earth; the pledge and cue
> Of a full feast; and the out-courts of glory!

How did the Christian Sunday come to be? We do not know the exact steps in the development; but we can surmise something of its origin from our knowledge of Christian worship in the age of the Apostles. The Jewish Sabbath extended from what we call Friday evening until Saturday evening. The earliest disciples would share that day in worship at the synagogue with their Jewish brethren. But at sundown on Saturday, when the Sabbath was past, they repaired to their homes for Christian prayers and the breaking of bread. When the Church's mission passed from Jewry to the Gentile world, Saturday evening, and on into the dawn of Sunday, was already fixed as the normal time for weekly gatherings. When the membership of the Church became predominantly Gentile, and all ties with the synagogue were broken, the first day of the week remained as the day of Christian worship. This change must have taken place before the death of the Apostles.[8] It would take no stretch of imagination for these Gentile Christians to see in their weekly meetings on Sundays a recalling of the Resurrection.

From time to time in the Church's history various groups

---

[8] See Acts 20:7; 1 Cor. 16:2.

have attempted to make Sunday into something akin to the Jewish Sabbath, with minute rules as to what should and what should not be done on this day. Such zeal is misdirected. No argument is needed as to the practical advantages of one day of rest each week. And there is a moral fitness in the reverent use of a holy day. Every day, however, no less than Sunday, is for a Christian a day to be spent to God's glory and the service of our fellow men. Sunday is our special glory, for on this day of days we remember in corporate worship what great things the Lord has done for us.

SAINT'S DAYS

The strength of our Easter faith is strikingly exhibited in the way the Christian fellowship remembers in prayer its faithful departed members. For each one of us there are two dates that mark our place in the mysterious order of time: the day of our birth, and the day of our death. So long as we live in the body on this earth we mark our birthdays as significant signposts of our growth in wisdom and grace. But in baptism we have been reborn to a timeless, eternal destiny, which we enter when death opens to us gates of larger life. The day we die is the day that marks our victory over sin and Satan and even death itself. Hence this is a day of high significance for the brotherhood of believers, the day when one of its members enters into the unending joy of his Lord, in sure and certain hope of resurrection unto eternal life.

In its liturgy the Church has always commemorated the day of a Christian's death to time, rather than the day of his birth in time. It has called this day of departure our "birthday in eternity." From the earliest times local parishes have recalled these anniversaries in their common prayers or in a Requiem celebration of the Eucharist. In order, however, to observe our unity and solidarity of fellowship throughout the whole Church one day is set aside each year when all our faithful departed are remembered —namely, All Saints' Day.

In the New Testament all Christians are called "saints." But in the course of time popular usage tended to restrict the term to those members of the Body who have especially distinguished themselves by their witness to Christ, whether by a martyr's death or by their service to His cause and to His lowly brethren. They represent to the whole Church treasured examples of what life enflamed with the love of God can be. Our Prayer Book Calendar does not exhaust the number of such saints. Indeed it gives us only a very select list of them, the apostles and evangelists of New Testament times. But for others that we may wish to commemorate the Prayer Book provides a Collect, Epistle and Gospel for their anniversaries (pp. 258-59).

Our Anglican Communion has never adopted the complex machinery employed in the Roman Catholic Church for formally "canonizing" a saint, i.e., solemnly proclaiming such and such a person to be worthy of a public commemoration in the Church's worship. We are content with the large liberty of local and provincial churches, exercised since ancient times, in drawing up their own lists of saints whose lives have been especially meaningful to them. Such local calendars have also contained other entries of particular interest—anniversaries of the dedication of churches, the dates of consecration of bishops, the transfer of relics of saints from neighboring churches or from one resting place to another.

The actual dates of the saint's days in our Prayer Book are derived from the calendar of the Roman Church, since, as we have seen, [9] the Roman liturgy came to be universally observed in the Western Church during the Middle Ages. These dates have diverse origins. Some of them, such as St. Andrew's Day, depend upon a tradition of the saint's day of martyrdom. Some go back to the day of consecration of churches at Rome in their honor, such as SS. Philip and James' Day on May 1st. Some are borrowed from the usages of other churches, such as the feast of the Conversion of St. Paul.

Of all the saint's days in the Prayer Book the earliest one that we can trace is St. Peter's Day on June 29th. It was instituted at Rome in the year 258, during a severe persecution of the Church. Originally, it was a day devoted to the memory of both St. Peter and St. Paul. Whether it represents some tradition of the day of their martyrdom, or whether it marks the transfer of their bodies at that time to a safe place of hiding, we do not know. What is important for us now is that we set aside a day to live again with Peter, as with all the saints, his devotion to his Lord, his sufferings in His service, and his triumph over death.[10]

THE "COMING" OF THE WORD MADE FLESH

In addition to the primary Easter cycle of holy days the Christian Year has another group of observances whose

---

[9] See Chapter IV.
[10] For the origins of the various saint's days, see M. H. Shepherd, Jr., *The Oxford American Prayer Book Commentary*, New York: Oxford University Press, 1950, pp. 226 ff.

focus is the twelve-day festival of the Incarnation from Christmas Day to the Epiphany. There is an interesting contrast in the respective origins of the two cycles. The Easter festival is the fulfilling and supplanting of the older Jewish Passover. Its date is movable, because it depends as the Passover did upon the lunar calendar, specifically the time of the first full moon after the spring equinox. Christmas and Epiphany, on the other hand, owe their origin to the Church's efforts to supplant by a Christian observance popular Gentile feasts of the birthdays of saviour-gods of heathenism. Such days were fixed and immovable, their date depending on the solar year. Thus the Christian Year, in its historical development, parallels the actual history of the spread of Christianity, first in its preaching of the gospel among the Jews, then among the Gentiles. It reminds us how the Christian faith has brought together and transformed the highest religious aspirations of all peoples, "where there is neither Greek nor Jew, circumcision nor uncircumcision . . . but Christ is all, and in all" (Col. 3:11).

As early as the beginning of the third century Christian groups in Egypt celebrated on January 6th a festival of the "Manifestation" in the world of our Redeemer Lord. The day was chosen in order to supplant a "manifestation" or birthday festival of the pagans in honor of the Egyptian saviour-god Osiris. From Egypt the Epiphany feast spread to all the Churches in the East. By the middle of the fourth century it was generally observed also throughout the Western Church. The "manifestation" theme was not restricted to one particular event in our Lord's life upon earth. It was related to various significant moments of His appearance among men as the Word made flesh—His birth,

His baptism, His first miracle at Cana of Galilee, and so forth.[11] Later in the Western Church, the Epiphany came to be peculiarly associated with St. Matthew's story of the visit of the Magi to the infant Christ. This story above all others seemed to symbolize in a dramatic way the full implication of our Lord's coming into the world in substance of our mortal flesh. He came to be the Saviour and Redeemer of all men everywhere, "to them that are far off and to them that are nigh." To Him all rulers and sages of the earth, with their kingdoms and possessions, shall come to acknowledge His Lordship.

With a somewhat similar purpose the church in Rome inaugurated Christmas Day in the early years of the fourth century. The date of December 25th was chosen not because of any tradition or memory of the exact time of our Lord's birth, but because of a definite desire to offset the great pagan festival of the Unconquered Sun. The most serious rival to Christianity in the West in the fourth century was the pagan cult of the Sun, a vague sort of monotheism that gathered about it many elements from older pagan traditions. Constantine had been attached to this religious devotion before his conversion to Christ. And it is thought by some scholars that Constantine may have been the one who originally suggested the institution of Christmas.

The chief festival of the Sun-cult was the winter solstice, reckoned in the fourth century as occurring on December 25th (not as today on December 21st). At this time the sun in its course begins to increase its light again and days become longer with its illumination. That there is a real

---

[11] Note how these manifestations of our Lord are recalled in the successive Gospels appointed for the Epiphany season; Prayer Book, pp. 108 ff.

connection of thought between this pagan festival and the new Christian observance is suggested by the opening of the most ancient collect for Christmas in the old Roman service books: "O God, who hast made this most holy night to shine with the illumination of the true light." Indeed the theme of "true light" runs through many of the ancient propers of the liturgy during the Christmas-Epiphany season. Thus devotion to Christ, the "Sun of Righteousness" [12] supplanted the cult of the Unconquered Sun of the heavenly luminaries.

Both the Eastern and Western Churches adopted each other's Incarnation and Manifestation feasts in the course of the fourth and fifth centuries. But the predominant influence of the Roman liturgy in the West has given to our tradition a greater interest in Christmas Day. Thus a series of other holy days related to the Incarnation theme have derived their dates from December 25th: the Annunciation, nine months before Christmas; the Nativity of St. John the Baptist, six months before Christmas; and the Presentation of our Lord in the Temple (also known as the Purification of St. Mary), forty days after Christmas. It should be noted that although popular devotion has accounted some of these days as festivals of St. Mary, they are primarily feasts of our Lord. The reverence and honor that are properly due to our Lord's mother are subordinate to the singular and unique worship that we offer to Him, of whose Incarnation she was blessed in being the humble and obedient instrument.

The feasts of our Lord's Nativity and Epiphany had such an impact upon the devotion of the Western Church

---

[12] Mal. 4:2. Cf. the word "day-spring" in the *Benedictus* (verse 11) of Morning Prayer, Prayer Book, p. 14.

that a season of penitential preparation for them was developed, somewhat similar to the Lenten preparation for Easter. In the Gallican churches the Epiphany, like Easter, became a stated time for baptisms. By the turn of the fifth century they had instituted a forty-day fast, on the analogy of Lent, prior to the Epiphany. When Rome adopted this "Advent" season in the sixth century, it reduced the length of the period to the four Sundays before Christmas, and modified the strictly penitential emphasis with more joyous notes in the singing of Alleluia.[13]

The word Advent literally means "Coming." Originally it applied to the whole cycle of commemoration of our Lord's first coming into the world—to Christmas and Epiphany no less than to the preparatory season. Throughout this period we join with the prophets of old in looking forward to the coming birth of the world's Redeemer. But it is not merely a historic "coming" in the manger crib of Bethlehem that we await, but His birth here and now within our hearts—so admirably expressed in Phillips Brooks' familiar carol:

> O holy child of Bethlehem!
> Descend to us, we pray;
> Cast out our sin, and enter in,
> Be born in us to-day.

Moreover we make ready for a greater Advent yet to come, when our Lord shall appear at the end of the world to be

---

[13] A reminder of the longer "Gallican" Advent remains in our Prayer Book, in the distinctly Advent character of the Sunday next before Advent, and in a lesser degree in the propers for the Fifth and Sixth Sundays after Epiphany, which are sometimes used after the 24th Sunday after Trinity. See Prayer Book, pp. 224-25.

our Judge, His last great Epiphany "with power and great glory" at the day of the general Resurrection.[14]

It is in this larger, richer context of "Advent" that the Christmas cycle and the Easter cycle of the Christian Year come together to proclaim one and the same gospel. For the Lord who comes in weakness is the same Lord who comes in power. The God made manifest in Mary's son, "of the seed of David according to the flesh," is the same who is "declared to be the Son of God with power . . . by the resurrection from the dead" (Rom. 1:3-4). In the Incarnation we behold the dignity of our nature, made in the image of God, but untainted by our sin. In the Resurrection and Ascension we see the glorious hope and destiny of our nature, re-made again after His likeness, out of great suffering and tribulation, that we should no more be the servants of sin. On Christmas Day the Western Church reads the same Gospel lesson at the Eucharist that the Eastern Church reads on Easter Day: the prologue of the Gospel of John: "And the Word was made flesh, and dwelt among us (and we beheld his glory, the glory as of the only begotten of the Father), full of grace and truth."

THE TRINITY SEASON

The drama of the Christian Year, celebrating the mighty acts of God for man's redemption, runs from Advent Sunday to Whitsunday. But there are almost as many weeks remaining after Whitsunday before Advent begins again. This long period, covering the summer and autumn months, is distinguished only by the recurring Sundays, which commemorate Easter, and a few fixed saint's days

---

[14] Note the similarity of the Gospels for the Second Sunday in Advent and the Sixth Sunday after the Epiphany; Prayer Book, pp. 93 and 118.

or holy days, such as the Transfiguration and All Saints. In the liturgical tradition of the Western Church, from the time of Alcuin, it was called simply the season "After Pentecost." It symbolized the long life of the historic Church, set between the first Pentecost which gave it birth and the final Advent at the end of history.

In the tenth century the first Sunday after Pentecost was transformed into a special feast in honor of the Blessed Trinity. In this way a fitting conclusion to the drama of the Christian Year was sought, by celebrating the ultimate revelation of God's being and nature as He is throughout all eternity. In England the festival became popular through its association with St. Thomas Becket, who was consecrated Archbishop of Canterbury on Trinity Sunday, in the year 1162.[15] The devotion of the people to Becket's memory in the later Middle Ages is responsible for the English tradition that names the Sundays after Pentecost as Sundays after Trinity.

It is commonly said that the twofold division of the year into the Advent-Whitsuntide cycle and the Trinity season gives us a valuable balance of emphasis. In the first half of the year we concentrate our attention upon our Lord's life, in the second half upon His teaching. Charles Wheatly, whose commentary on the Prayer Book was a classic manual for almost two centuries, put it this way: "The whole year is distinguished into two parts: the design of the first being to commemorate Christ's living amongst us; the other to instruct us to live after his example." [16]

---

[15] On Thomas Becket, see *Chapters in Church History*, pp. 115-18.
[16] *A Rational Illustration of the Book of Common Prayer*, V. vii. 5. Wheatly's work was first published in 1710, and several times enlarged. I quote from the Bohn Library reprint of 1850.

Such statements contain, undoubtedly, an element of truth, and as broad generalizations they may have some value. But we cannot divorce our Lord's life from His teaching, nor can we commemorate His life properly without applying its lessons to ourselves. Even an ordinary Sunday, as we have seen, commemorates an extraordinary event. And a parable, or a story from our Lord's life, read on such an ordinary Sunday reveals to us One who came among us a Saviour and Redeemer. The less dramatic character of the Trinity season has an important place in the total scheme of things. It gives us time to digest more thoroughly the primary lessons and truths of the Advent-Whitsuntide cycle, and thus prepares us at the same time for the coming of our Saviour and Judge anew in all His glorious appearing. We live, through our liturgical year, literally between two worlds, marked by the two Advents of our Lord, His coming to us in time and His coming to us for all eternity.

CHAPTER SIX

Morning and Evening Prayer and the Litany

I<small>N OUR</small> ordinary usage we have come to refer to all the services of the Prayer Book as "Common Prayer." But if one examines the title page of the Prayer Book closely it will be noted that a distinction is made between "Common Prayer" and the "Sacraments and Other Rites and Ceremonies of the Church." This distinction has a historical basis. The sacraments and other occasional rites are liturgies given us by our Lord or by official action of the Church. Their essential elements are fixed. But the "Common Prayer" of the Church, in the strict sense of the term, directly stems from the spontaneous devotions of Christian people. Though the Church officially selects, modifies and sanctions these devotions, they remain essentially liturgies of the laity. They do not require the ministry of ordained clergy.

The "Common Prayer" includes specifically the daily offices of Morning and Evening Prayer, and the Litany. These services have been distilled from a vast reservoir of experience in praise, meditation and prayer in the daily lives of God's people, both Jewish and Christian. Much of their inspiration and contents have sprung from the private devotions of individuals. But the offices have, in their turn, greatly enriched the substance of personal prayer and praise. Above everything else, they guide our worship of God away from self-centered and eccentric devotions, and place us in the broad, deep courses of the Church's corporate thirsting after God.

The daily offices fulfill a dual purpose in our common Christian life. They provide us with a regular discipline, day by day, year in and year out, for offering together our homage to God for His creation and preservation of us and for all the blessings of this life. They are, first of all, acts of adoration. By means of them we join in that unceasing chorus whereby the whole creation, both the things visible and things invisible, responds in loving dependence upon its Maker. Secondly, the offices bring God's Word near to us. They teach us of God's continual favor towards us, His righteous purpose for us, and His just judgments upon us.

THE STRUCTURE OF THE OFFICES

In the opening Exhortation of the offices ("Dearly beloved brethren," Prayer Book, pp. 5-6, and 23) there is a succinct outline of the four principal parts of these services. We shall follow this outline. One should note, however, how finely balanced these four parts are, no one of them dominating the whole. Moreover they are so skillfully linked one with the other that we are not conscious of sudden and dramatic changes. Yet there is a distinct rhythm of movement in the contents of the offices. And they develop towards a focal climax.

1. The offices begin with a penitential introduction— "to acknowledge and confess our manifold sins and wickedness . . . to the end that we may obtain forgiveness of

the same." The opening Sentences of Scripture and the Exhortation are designed to set our hearts and minds upon the presence of a holy God, who comes to meet us in both love and judgment. The seasonal Sentences in particular recall the mighty acts of God on our behalf, or set us to think reflectively upon the purpose of these mighty acts both for ourselves and for the world. Our consciences are at once smitten. We recognize ourselves as "miserable sinners" indeed in His presence. We have broken faith with Him. Therefore, first of all, a rightful relation with God must be restored, by confessing our sin and receiving His forgiveness.

The clue to this section of the offices is the troublesome phrase in the General Confession: "there is no health in us." The word "health" here has nothing to do with our physical, or even our spiritual well-being, though obviously we are not in a state of "wholeness" because of our sin. Modern medicine is reminding us today of a truth that our Lord knew full well; namely, that spiritual disorder and sin affect very definitely the health of the body. The word "health" in this context, however, means "saving health." That is to say, we do not have within ourselves the capacity of making ourselves whole. We cannot of our own power undo the mischief that sin has worked in us. Only in God is there "saving health." Only God can forgive sin and restore us to wholeness and a right relation to Himself. And this He does "in Christ Jesus our Lord." [1] Hence in the Absolution said by the priest, we are reminded that God's forgiveness comes only to those who both "truly repent" and "unfeignedly believe his holy Gospel"—the good news of our Lord's redemption.

---

[1] See *The Faith of the Church*, pp. 71-77.

But there is more to receive than forgiveness alone. The Absolution goes on to remind us that we seek also the Holy Spirit, both for our present worship and for the rest of our lives, that we may ultimately come to the crowning blessing of "eternal joy." Thus if we ponder closely the words of this penitential introduction we find ourselves reaching out to contemplate the whole mystery of our Christian Faith, in all its fullness and glory. We find our right relationship to all three Persons of the Blessed Trinity. We glimpse the depth of God's love in the Incarnation and Atonement of His Son. We reach after the final prize that all this love offers us—eternal life and joy.

The Lord's Prayer brings to a close this introductory liturgy of confession and absolution. Assured of God's grace and help, we can say it now with pure intent and loving fervor. Brief versicles, asking God's help, lead us to the next part of our service, the psalms of praise.

2. The Psalter forms the second section of the offices— "to render thanks for the great benefits that we have received at his hands, to set forth his most worthy praise." At Morning Prayer the *Venite* (Psalm 95:1-7 and 96:9,13) usually introduces the psalmody and sets the keynote for all our praise.[2] Surrounding all the Psalms, as it were a frame, is the doxology to the Trinity, the *Gloria Patri*. This serves both to remind us of Him to whom our praises are addressed, and also to give a Christian interpretation to the Psalms.

Not all the Psalms, of course, are hymns of praise and thanksgiving. Some are penitential. Some are prayers for

---

[2] The *Venite* may be omitted when Psalm 95 is used, and on the fast days of Ash Wednesday and Good Friday. Substitutes for the *Venite* are provided for Easter week and Thanksgiving Day. (Prayer Book, pp. 8, 162-63, 264-65.)

God's help in trying times and circumstances. Others are recitals of the history of Israel, or meditations upon the Old Testament Law. A few of them are "complaints" addressed to God, and at times they break forth in unseemly cries for vengeance upon enemies. The variety both of material and of mood in the Psalter lends to it a fascinating interest. It also makes the Psalter a supreme resource for worship. For the worshipper finds in its words every kind of response to God and to the world about him.[3] Rowland Prothero, in his familiar classic, *The Psalms in Human Life,* said that the Psalms "are a mirror in which each man sees the motions of his own soul." It is a mirror, too, of the aspirations of a people. For even the most personal of the Psalms is readily expressive of the commonfelt "devices and desires" of all human hearts.

Many people have difficulty with the Psalms, none the less, because they do not always express the highest Christian sentiments. We should not expect an ancient Hebrew hymn book composed centuries before the coming of Christ to refer specifically to the mysteries of our faith in Him. In particular, the Psalms do not always give a profound answer to the problem of suffering, and they do not speak in clear accents about eternal life. At times they seem shallow and unreal in their optimistic view of rewards for the innocent and dire punishments for the wicked. Some Psalms appear to exhibit an unattractive self-righteousness and lack of humility. Then there are the terrible "cursings" of oppressors and enemies, so far removed from our Lord's teaching about the need of love for those who persecute and despitefully use us. The Prayer Book allows many of these passages in the Psalms to be omitted in

---

[3] See *The Holy Scriptures,* pp. 95-97.

public worship; but it is difficult to extricate all of them without causing confusion.[4]

There is no reason to gloss over these objections to the Psalter. Oftentimes we can make some verses edifying only by a deliberate rejection of their literal meaning. The enemies of Israel must be understood, for us at least, as "spiritual" forces of evil that contend against us. But these problems of the Psalter are far outweighed by two of its virtues. One is the absolute honesty and sincerity of the Psalms. They do not make any effort to "dissemble or cloak" any thoughts or feelings "before the face of Almighty God." They bring everything out into the open. We, too, like the psalmists, have many evil thoughts and imaginations. If we, like them, will only bring them out into the searching light of God's holiness and justice, we shall the more easily let them wither and die in the burning heat of His love. The other virtue of the Psalms is their attitude of unfailing trust in God. No matter how desperate the circumstances of which the Psalmist complains, he is always trustful of God's concern for him and of His ultimate victory over the powers of evil. Sincerity and trust—these are the basic requirements of all true worship. The Psalter expresses these fundamental attitudes in a supreme degree. And out of these qualities come its many other virtues—joy and delight in God and in His worship, thanksgiving for His provident mercies and loving-kindness, and keen devotion to the keeping of His commandments.

There is a deeper reason also why the Psalter should

[4] Many Psalms, as printed in the Prayer Book, have unsuitable verses set off in paragraphs that can easily be omitted. Note also that the lectionary on pages x ff. frequently provides for only a selection of verses from some of the Psalms.

be the staple of Christian worship. The Church has from its earliest days considered the Psalter a prophetic book. It summarizes the history and devotion of God's chosen people of old, and thus prefigures the life of Him who fulfilled their call to obedience. Our Lord Himself used the Psalms continually in His own life of prayer and praise. If we who belong to His Body would share to the full the self-offering of His life to the Father, we must learn to pray as He prayed, to sing as He sang. And this can only be done if the Church takes His devotion for its own and meditates upon the Psalms which nourished and sustained Him, even to the hours of bitter anguish upon the Cross.

3. The third section of the offices leads us into the revelation of God's mighty acts for our redemption, by the hearing of "his most holy Word." We have already discussed in an earlier chapter [5] the significance of the reading of Holy Scripture in our worship. At this point we would remind ourselves again that the purpose of the lessons from the Bible is not merely to instruct us in the history of God's saving acts for His people. God's Word brings us into communion with His presence. The lessons are also acts of praise, and are read to the glory of God. They continue the praise of the Psalms, which are themselves a part of Scripture. And the canticles which follow each lesson give the proper context for their reading.

In the course of a year the daily offices introduce us to the contents of the entire Bible. If one will examine the tables on pages x-xlv of the Prayer Book, it will be seen that the several books are read, at least on weekdays, in a regular sequence. But we do not read them straight through, from Genesis to Revelation. The books are distributed

---

[5] See Chapter II.

according to their general appropriateness to the themes of the seasons of the Christian Year. For example, Isaiah and Revelation are read in Advent, because the former records the chief prophecies of the coming of the Messiah, the latter portrays in vivid pictures the second coming of the Lord at the end of time. At Evening Prayer, during Lent, we read the prophet Jeremiah, whose poignant laments over the sin of Israel incite us to repentance. Beginning in Septuagesima we read Genesis and Exodus (at Morning Prayer) in such a way that we are brought to the story of the first Passover by Easter Day, when "Christ our Passover is sacrificed for us." [6]

Just as in the case of the Psalms, so also in the lessons, especially those appointed from the Old Testament, we come upon many particular lessons that seem unedifying or unsuitable to Christian worship. But again, we must exercise our imaginations to see the drama of sacred history as a whole. The story of the New Testament is continuous with the story of the Old. [7] We cannot understand the fuller revelation given to the Church unless we know the partial revelation given to Israel. We see our own spiritual progress reflected in the triumphs and defeats, the joys and humiliations of God's people. We learn the degradation that is the result of sin, and the sure hope of glory that is the reward of faith and patient obedience. Unless we have the whole sweep of Bible history presented to us, we miss the full relevance of its central, unifying theme—how God has wrought from the faith of Abraham

---

[6] One will find an excellent discussion of the *rationale* of our Office lectionary in Bayard H. Jones, *The American Lectionary*, New York: Morehouse-Gorham Co., 1944.

[7] See *The Holy Scriptures*, Chapter I.

and his seed, "in the house of his servant David," a mighty salvation for us in the Person of Jesus Christ.

The canticles that follow the lessons are all, with the exception of the *Te Deum,* drawn from Scripture. Even the *Te Deum* is a mosaic of scriptural quotation and allusion, and the finest summary, outside the Bible, of the faith the Bible teaches. The *Benedictus es* and the *Benedicite* are parts of one continuous hymn of praise to God as the sovereign Lord of all creation. They are taken from the *Song of the Three Children* in the Old Testament Apocrypha.[8] The psalm-canticles, the *Jubilate* and the psalms appointed at Evening Prayer, express the joy of God's people in their worship of Him, a note so characteristic of the Psalter as a whole. The favorite canticles of the Church throughout the ages have been the "Gospel canticles"—the *Benedictus, Magnificat* and *Nunc Dimittis.* They are hymns celebrating the coming of the Messiah. They proclaim the hope of the Old Testament as it finds its fulfillment in the New. In Evening Prayer, especially, the Gospel canticles lend to this section of the office a climactic development. The *Magnificat* sums up the promise of the Old Testament as it looks forward to the Incarnation. The *Nunc Dimittis* views the Incarnation as accomplished and draws out the full implications of it both for Israel and for the Gentile peoples.

With the canticles after the New Testament lesson we reach the dramatic climax of the daily offices. The final revelation of God has been made known to us. We thereupon bring this section of the offices to a close in reciting the Creed. For the Creed also serves as a summary of the mighty acts of God for our salvation, revealed to us in the

---

[8] For a discussion of the Apocrypha, see *ibid.,* pp. 20-21 and 74.

Holy Scriptures.[9] But the Creed is much more than a summary statement. It is a profession of our own faith. It commits us to that saving Word we have just received. It reminds us day after day of the basic pledge of our lives, the faith we professed at our Baptism when we were made living members of Christ's Body, the Church. Note, too, how at this point the offices become intensely individual. Heretofore we have been speaking as a group, using plural pronouns. Now the pronoun changes to the first person singular—"*I* believe." Each worshipper becomes personally responsible, so to speak, for the common allegiance.

4. The final section of the offices consists of the prayers, wherein we "ask those things which are requisite and necessary, as well for the body as the soul." It is significant that these prayers of petition are placed at the end of the services, after we have offered our praise to God and received His Word. For only in the perspective of all that has preceded them can these prayers be rightfully made. If we have not thought first about the nature of God and His purposes for us, we are not prepared to ask anything of Him "according to his will." [10]

The prayers begin with a brief series of verses from the Psalms, said responsively between minister and people. They summon God's aid in our prayers that we may ask our petitions by the help of His grace and Spirit. These versicles and responses form a "little litany" and gather together the themes of the prayers that follow. Such forms are very characteristic of liturgical worship; for they are of great assistance in making our prayers truly corporate.

---

[9] See *The Faith of the Church*, pp. 10-13.
[10] See Chapter II.

There follows three prescribed collects,[11] and after these, the minister may finish the prayers in several ways. He may close at once with the Grace, or he may add any or all of the prayers printed in the offices themselves. He may also use the Litany, or any other prayers and devotions among the many provided by the Prayer Book. In this way the offices can be adapted concretely to the immediate needs of our day-to-day lives. The prayers are always concluded with the Grace (2 Cor. 13:14), a benediction recalling the three Persons of the Blessed Trinity. Thus our prayers end, as our praises began, with God's Name upon our lips.

The three prescribed collects of the offices are, in themselves, a complete summary of the Church's continual prayer to God. The Collect for the Day links the offices both with the Holy Communion and with the full-rounded cycle of themes of the Christian Year. Its use here also suggests that the daily offices are in fact the Church's corporate preparation for the Holy Communion, and a sustaining, devotional commentary upon that central act of worship. The Collects for Peace, at both Morning and Evening Prayer, are general petitions for God's protection of His Church "at all times and in all places." They presuppose the fact that so long as the Church exists in a world of sin and strife, it will be beset by many enemies, both

---

[11] The word "collect" means "gathered together." Originally the word referred to the assembled congregation, but later it was used to connote the "gathering together" of the people's prayers. The form of the collect comes to us from the Roman liturgy. It consists of four parts: 1) an opening address to God, often with some clause that states an attribute of His nature or activity; 2) a single petition, with a statement of the result to be obtained by the granting of the petition; 3) a pleading in Christ's Name; and 4) a concluding doxology. In many of the Prayer Book Collects the Doxology is omitted.

material and spiritual, that seek to destroy its peace and safety. Similarly, the Collects for Grace and for Aid against Perils apply this petition to the very present day and hour in which our worship is set.

These prayers are not, as some have imagined, a plea for escape from the world and all its dangers to the body and the soul. They are rather an earnest supplication that we may not be anxious about them, "that we, surely trusting in [God's] defence, may not fear the power" of any enemies. For we know the might of God's victory over sin in our Lord Jesus Christ, and the peace that comes to those whose trust and obedience are rooted in His will—a peace indeed "which the world cannot give."

THE BACKGROUND OF THE OFFICES

The daily offices of Morning and Evening Prayer have been described as the greatest single liturgical achievement of the English Reformers, and of Archbishop Cranmer in particular. The clearest testimony to that achievement is the way these forms of worship have taken hold of the devotion of the people in our Anglican communion these past four hundred years. The richness and depth of their contents have satisfied the aspirations of all sorts of people. The simplicity of their structure and the large element of fixed and unvarying forms make them admirably suited to popular use and corporate participation. At the same time they provide such variety in psalmody, lessons and prayer, that constant and repeated use fails to make them monotonous or dull. There is always some new insight that they awaken in us by reason of the variable combinations of Old and New Testament materials.

Yet, strange as it may seem, there was nothing contained in the offices, as they were shaped by Cranmer's hands, that had not been part of the Church's daily worship for a thousand years. Only the penitential introduction, added to the second Prayer Book of 1552, was composed at the time of the Reformation. The materials of the offices, from the versicle, "O Lord, open thou our lips," through the third of the prescribed collects, were all taken from the medieval breviary services that the clergy and monks, and some of the laity, had been saying and singing since ancient times.

For Morning Prayer Cranmer took elements from the old canonical hours of Matins, Lauds, and Prime; for Evening Prayer he combined materials from Vespers and Compline.[12] By reducing the old system from eight offices to two he returned to the simpler schedule of the ancient Church. It is true that many devout Christians of early times kept "hours of prayer" at other times than the beginning and end of the day. But these were private devotions, until the monks developed them into corporate, choir offices. But morning and evening prayers were observed publicly, as early as the fourth century—if not every day, at least on Wednesdays and Fridays. The laity participated in them so long as they understood the language. By rendering the offices into the vernacular, Cranmer again restored to the laity their ancient privilege of taking an active part in the Church's daily devotions.

The offices have undergone some revision and supplementation since the Reformation. We have noted that the penitential introduction was added in 1552. The prayers after the third collect are contributions of the 1661 Book

---

[12] See Chapter IV.

and later revisions. Thus every age in the history of Christian devotion has made a contribution to our common, daily prayers. The Psalms and the Lord's Prayer formed the substance of the offices in the apostolic age. The Creed comes to us from the second century; the *Te Deum* is the flower of the Church's hymnody in the great age of the fathers of the fourth and fifth century. The seasonal anthems used with the *Venite* (called "invitatory antiphons") are reminders of the rich variety and splendor of medieval worship, while the invariable Collects for Peace and Aid recall the dark ages of barbarian settlements in Western Europe following upon the collapse of the Roman Empire. The General Confession represents the scriptural piety of the Reformers, and the prayer for All Conditions of Men and the General Thanksgiving were written in the seventeenth century. Last of all, the alternative prayer for the President in Morning Prayer ("O Lord, our Governor") was composed in our own times for inclusion in the revised American Prayer Book of 1928. No doubt generations to come will make their contributions to the common heritage. But the core of the offices will always remain what it has been through the ages—God's praise in psalmody and hymn, God's Word in Holy Scripture, God's aid and defense in suppliant prayer.

THE LITANY

The Litany (Prayer Book, pp. 54-59) is a particular form of common prayer, consisting of biddings or petitions by a leader followed by brief responses of the people. The form was used by both Jews and pagans in ancient times; and the Church took it over and developed it in the fourth century. Litanies may express all kinds of worshipful attitudes, praise, penitence, petition. In the Middle Ages litanies invoking the aid of the saints were popular, and such litanies are still used in the Roman Catholic Church. Our Prayer Book Litany is descended from a special form used in the Middle Ages, either separately, or in combination with the offices or the Eucharist.

The Litany is actually the oldest part of the Prayer Book, for it was first issued in the year 1544, during the reign of King Henry VIII. Cranmer did not content himself with a mere translation of the medieval form. He condensed and adapted it, adding to it suggestions derived from litanies in the Eastern Orthodox liturgy and the German litany set forth by Luther in 1529. All successive revisions of the Prayer Book have added or subtracted phrases and petitions. Like the daily offices, the Litany provides us with an epitome of Christian supplication through the ages. In one of its petitions, for example, we pray for "all prisoners and captives," a phrase that comes down from the first days of persecution, and in the same breath we pray for all who travel by air.

Analysis of the Litany reveals it to be made up of five parts. All but the first of these, the invocations of the Holy Trinity, are addressed directly to our Lord. The invocations originally included addresses to the saints, but these were all eliminated in the first Prayer Book. The invocations remind us that prayer always begins with adoration, and that adoration always involves penitence. The second and third parts are printed in the Prayer Book as one continuous section. These are the deprecations—prayers that we may be delivered from all evil, both material and spiritual; and the obsecrations, a series of entreaties recalling all our Lord's redemptive work for us.

The suffrages, or petitions, make up the fourth and largest part of the Litany. Most of them are intercessions for all sorts and conditions of men; but the last two petitions are prayers for our physical and spiritual well-being. A brief series of intense cries to our Lord for His mercy lead into the Lord's Prayer. At this point the Litany may be concluded by passing to the final prayer. But a fifth section is provided, of a strongly penitential character. It is based upon a special intercession in the medieval Litany, for use in time of war.

The power of the Litany as a popular devotion, whether said quietly on our knees or sung in solemn procession, is not due simply to its matchless grace of style and rhythm. It has this in supreme degree, to any ear that is sensitive to the music of our English tongue. The Litany grips us because it faces squarely the tragedy of life in suffering and need, whether due to human sin or to natural evils over which we have no control. It faces tragedy without fear and without despair. For pervading its whole course of supplication is an unconquerable trust in the mercy and power of God to redeem and to save. It knows that God Himself in the Person of His Son has faced the "agony and bloody sweat" of Cross and Passion, and that out of tribulation He has come to a glorious Resurrection and Ascension. Even in our final, naked loneliness of death's inevitable hour, and in the searching scrutiny of the day of judgment, He will arise and spare us, and deliver us for His Name's sake.

THE IMPORTANCE OF THE OFFICES

The daily offices and the Litany are not essential to the Church's life in the sense that the sacraments are. Baptism incorporates us into Christ's Body and the Holy Communion sustains and nourishes us as members of His Body in a way that is unique. They allow of no substitutes. But the non-sacramental services marvelously enrich our life in Him, and in truth they do much to determine the quality of that life. For by the practice and use of them, "the people," said Archbishop Cranmer in his preface to the first Prayer Book, "should continually profit more and more in the knowledge of God, and be the more inflamed with the love of his true religion." Nor should we forget that many persons have been drawn to this knowledge and love of God by means of the offices themselves, before they have experienced other liturgies of the Church. Indeed, when supplemented with sermon, offering and hymns, as is so commonly done on Sundays and other days, the offices are effective both as a means of our communion with God, and as a common education and discipline in our faith and obedience to His holy Word.

The Church is obliged to celebrate and administer the sacraments. We are commanded so to do by our Lord. The obligation resting upon us to observe the daily offices is of a different sort. It does not arise from obedience to a direct command, but from an inward compunction of the spirit. We need to adore God, to repent of our sins, to learn of His truth, and to seek His help, day after day continually throughout our lives. It is not enough to lay the burden of this discipline upon our private, personal devotions. For these need always the corrective and perspective of the Church's corporate prayers. If we cannot conveniently assemble together in church each day to say the Church's daily prayers, we can join them no less, either in family worship or in setting aside some portion of our private devotions for these offices.

In certain medieval religious houses the monks felt so

keenly the importance of lifting not only themselves but also the entire world to God, in continual prayer and praise, that they arranged their daily routine to this end. The entire community would be divided into shifts, like workers in war production plants, for the work of worship. While part of the community was engaged in manual labor or in rest, another part would take their station in the chapel choir. Not an hour passed, by day or by night, without the voice of common praise and prayer going up to God from the midst of their common life.

Men, of course, cannot live like the angels, or even like many monks. We can certainly worship God by our daily lives no less than by our daily prayers. We glorify Him not only in hymns and chants but more especially in keeping His commandments. But if we set apart some portion of each morning and evening for His worship, we sanctify all our thoughts and endeavors, and lift them out of service of self into service of Him. Thus by these means of grace we "redeem the time" and seize with certain assurance the hope of glory.

CHAPTER SEVEN

The Holy Communion

THE CENTRAL ACT of Christian worship has been described by many titles. In the New Testament writings St. Paul calls it the Lord's Supper; the Book of Acts refers to it as the Breaking of Bread. There are also hints in the New Testament of the term Eucharist, which means Thanksgiving, the title by which the rite was generally known among the early Christians. Another ancient name for it is the Holy Mysteries. The Eastern Christians finally settled upon the use of the word Liturgy. In Western Catholicism a Latin word, *missa,* employed at first as a general term for liturgical offices, gradually took on a restricted meaning. From it is derived the word Mass. Literally the term *missa* refers to the "dismissals" at the end of the rite. Hence in popular usage, to stay "for the dismissal" came to mean "for the whole rite." The Latin Church has also contributed the titles Blessed Sacrament and Holy Sacrifice.

Our common Anglican terminology, since the Reformation, has fastened upon the phrase, the Holy Communion. This title was frequently used in early and medieval times to refer to the act of communion itself, within the rite.

Thus we also have taken a term which technically refers to one part of the service and made it refer to the whole.[1]

All of these historic titles have their value in emphasizing important aspects and meanings of the sacrament. Yet none of them fully describes its whole wealth of significance. Perhaps no one term can, except in so far as we read into it all the meanings that we wish it to convey. Our best approach to an understanding of the Holy Communion, however, will not be by way of its many titles, but by a consideration of what our Lord Himself said and did at the Last Supper.

THE LAST SUPPER

It is not necessary to discuss here the debated question whether the supper our Lord shared with His disciples on the last evening of His earthly life was or was not the Passover meal.[2] In any event the sacred associations of the Passover festival must have been uppermost in the hearts and minds of those who gathered with Jesus in the Upper Room. It was a vivid remembrance of God's deliverance of His people from oppression and bondage in Egypt, and the covenant God made with them, after they had passed through the Red Sea and set upon their journey to the land that He promised to give them. In the tense atmosphere of first century Palestine each new Passover festival revived eager longings for a new and final deliverance from the oppression of the Roman Empire, and the establishment upon earth of God's everlasting Kingdom. A new covenant would then be made, as foretold by Jeremiah (31:31-34),

[1] The Prayer Book frequently uses the titles Lord's Supper and "holy mysteries." It also uses (once) the terms "breaking of bread" (p. 166), "blessed Sacrament" (pp. 294, 565), and "the holy Eucharist" (p. 574).

[2] See *The Holy Scriptures*, pp. 141-42.

when God would write His law upon their hearts, and all His people would know and obey Him, "from the least of them unto the greatest of them," and their sin would be forgiven and remembered no more.[3]

These hopes of the disciples were centered upon their Master, whom they believed to be the Messiah promised of God to inaugurate the New Covenant and Kingdom. But they did not understand the true character of this Kingdom. It was not to be a realm of temporal power and dominion, but a sovereign rule of God in the lives of men, issuing in their lowly service one to another. Again and again our Lord had stressed this point, both in His parables about the Kingdom and in His deeds of loving-kindness to the needy and the outcasts of society. He had frequently used the picture of a banquet to express what the life of God's Kingdom was like, where the proud give place to the humble, and the over-privileged are replaced by the under-privileged. And in His own ministry He had won a reputation for His friendship with sinners. To the scandal of the self-righteous He would "eat and drink" with them, and in His love for them bring them to repentance and newness of life. So in His final words to His disciples at the Supper He reminded them that:

The kings of the Gentiles exercise lordship over them; and they that exercise authority upon them are called benefactors. But ye shall not be so: but he that is greatest among you, let him be as the younger; and he that is chief, as he that doth serve. (Luke 22:25-26.)

That a life so consecrated to God in service to men should lead to the supreme sacrifice of the Cross is the

---

[3] For the meaning of "covenant," see *ibid.*, pp. 105-108.

tragic revelation of the extent to which human sin can despise and reject the love of God. For this love our Lord "was contented to be betrayed, and given up into the hands of wicked men, and to suffer death upon the cross" (Prayer Book, p. 156). Yet by this love He broke the power of sin. By His broken body and outpoured blood He made possible the reconciliation of God and man. He did indeed inaugurate the new Covenant, and bring the hearts of all those who are united to Him by faith into loving obedience of God's sovereign rule in His Kingdom.

In order that we should always remember Him and what He has done for us, our Lord gave to His disciples the observance of the Supper, and commanded them to continue it. By "remembering" Him He did not mean a mere mental recollection of something past and done. To remember Him is to make Him present in our very midst. To remember Him means to be united to Him, by sharing in His self-offering, and thereby sharing also in His victory over sin. It means letting Him come in all the grace and power of His Holy Spirit and take authority over our whole lives, transforming them into His likeness and lifting them up to God. Thus when we take bread, bless, break and eat it, and take a cup of wine, and bless and drink of it, according to His institution "in remembrance of Him," we are by His promise made one with Him. For He said the Bread was His Body and the Wine was His Blood.

By identifying Himself with the blessed Bread and Wine, our Lord gave the disciples the sacrifice of the new Covenant, to be continually offered by God's new Israel, the Church. This does not mean that the blessed elements of Bread and Wine are themselves sacrificial offerings. Our Lord is not offered afresh every time we consecrate the elements according to His institution and command. He has made His offering entirely, once for all, on Calvary. The consecrated elements are the "memorial" of His sacrifice. They cannot repeat it, they only re-present it. And in the re-presenting of it, they make its benefits available to those who would receive them in penitence and faith and love, with thanksgiving.[4]

The Holy Supper of the Lord is also a sure pledge of our participation in the Kingdom of God. For surely if we are made one with Him we have a foretaste of that ultimate glory, when all who belong to Christ shall reign with Him because like Him they all serve God entirely. Our Lord Himself told His disciples at the Last Supper that when He broke bread and shared the cup with them again it would be in His Father's Kingdom. He did not mean by this promise that He would not be with them in this act of remembrance until the final end of the world, when He shall appear in power and great glory. He is present at every celebration of the Supper, present in His risen, life-giving Spirit, sacramentally in the Bread and Wine. In this action we "remember" Him not only in His Cross and Passion, but also in His mighty Resurrection and glorious Ascension. United to His Person, we are in a wonderful way lifted up into the heavenly places where He is Lord of all.

The New Testament tells us in several places that the risen Lord made Himself known to His disciples in the Breaking of Bread.[5] The Last Supper, with its impending tragedy, was thereby transformed into the Messianic Ban-

---

[4] See *The Faith of the Church*, pp. 150-55. For the offering of ourselves in sacrifice in this service, see pp. 156 ff.

[5] See especially Luke 24:30 ff., John 21:12-14, Acts 10:41.

quet of which He had said so much in His parables of the Kingdom. In the outpouring of His Spirit upon His Church the disciples knew themselves partakers of the age to come, and to "have tasted the heavenly gift" (Heb. 6:4-5). And in the loving fellowship of service one to another, now centered in the holy banquet Table, He had truly "exalted the humble and meek" and had "filled the hungry with good things." It is no wonder that they celebrated the Breaking of Bread, as the Book of Acts tells us, "with gladness, . . . praising God" (2:46), and that they came to speak of it as the Eucharist, "The Thanksgiving."

It was characteristic of the simplicity as also of the depth of our Lord's discernment that in leaving us a memorial of Himself, He should choose, not some strange and exotic ceremony, but an action universal in human experience— the family meal. He took the most obvious symbol of our common life and made it the supreme sacrament of His life. Food and drink are necessities of our physical existence. Bread is our very staff of life. (And we must remember that the widespread poverty of first century Palestine made the gift of "daily bread" God's greatest boon of all His material creation.) Wine is the symbol of life's joys and trials. The Old Testament refers to "the cup" in contexts of both gladness and sorrow. Bread and wine, however, must be made. They involve man's work upon the gifts of God's creation. They are thus symbols of our common life in all its social and economic relationships. The basic social unit is the family, living in mutual love and service. The family meal is therefore the most perfect parable of all man's creaturely relationships and needs.

Our Lord's disciples are His family. "Whosoever shall do the will of God," said He, "the same is my brother, and my sister, and mother" (Mark 3:35). So He used the final meal He shared on earth with His family as the sign and instrument for the formation of "the household of faith." And He said to them, in effect, that when they meet together in this fundamental relationship of life, in loving fellowship and in remembrance of Him, they are fulfilling the will of God and are thereby partakers of the Kingdom of heaven.

THE SACRAMENT IN THE CHURCH

We have traced in a preceding chapter[6] the broad outline of how the liturgy our Lord performed in the Upper Room has come down through the ages in the Eucharistic rite of the Church. We have noted that already by the middle of the second century the structure of the service had achieved a common form that underlies all the later historic rites of Christendom, East and West. Our Prayer Book rite is a direct descendant of the Western development of this common tradition. Yet it has some special features of its own. We have noted, too, how our American Prayer Book has combined both an English and a Scottish inheritance, and how, through the latter strain of its ancestry, it has been enriched with materials from the Eastern, no less than from the Western, rites.

Before engaging in an analysis of our Prayer Book rite, a few words should be given to the place the eucharistic sacrament has held in the common life of the Church through the centuries. From the earliest times the Holy Communion has always been celebrated on all Sundays and other holy days of the Church's calendar. It has also been celebrated on many special occasions, in every con-

---

[6] See Chapter IV.

ceivable context of Christian witness and life. It has sanctified marriages and burials, brought comfort to the anxious, the sick and the dying. It has been offered for the gift
of many blessings, spiritual and temporal: for peace, for
the conversion of the heathen, for travelers, and for a varied multitude of individual intentions or thanksgivings.
In the medieval Western Church it was celebrated every
day wherever there was a priest to serve at an altar, and in
many places it was celebrated several times a day.

It is sometimes supposed that the Protestant Reformers
of the sixteenth century opposed the frequent celebration
of the Eucharist. But this is not the case. What they opposed was the multiplying of celebrations without communion by the people. All the Reformers, except Zwingli,
insisted that the Holy Communion should be the principal
service every Sunday and major holy day. They were well
aware that this was the tradition and practice of the ancient
Church. They had no objection to celebrations on other
days, provided always that there were a "sufficient" number of persons to communicate with the priest. In their
strong emphasis upon the necessity of communion at every
celebration, they were reacting against real abuses of private and solitary masses that had grown up in the medieval
Church.

We must remember that during the long course of the
Middle Ages the laity received communion very infre-
quently, most of them doing so only once a year at Easter.
The Reformers' insistence upon communions at every celebration, as in the ancient Church, was little less than revo-
lutionary. The laity were not prepared for so radical a
change in their habits of devotion. Hence the Reformers
were forced to a compromise, which they did not alto-

gether desire. If there were no communions, there was to be no full celebration of the Eucharist. The minister was directed in such cases to conclude the service with a Blessing after the Ante-Communion.

Except in a few cathedrals and larger parish churches, the customary Sunday service in Anglicanism, after the Reformation, came to be Morning Prayer, Litany, Ante-Communion and sermon. The complete celebration of the Holy Communion was observed only four times a year, though in some places it was provided at least once a month. One of the most important results of the Catholic revival in the nineteenth century, commonly known as the Oxford Movement,[7] was the restoration of more frequent celebrations in the parishes, and an emphasis on more adequate preparation for participation in them. By the end of the century most parishes had a celebration of the Holy Communion every Sunday and holy day, as provided in the Prayer Book, and many of them had one or more celebrations during the week. But the Sunday celebration did not, in many places, become the "principal" parish service more than once a month. The variety in Sunday schedules of services which one finds today throughout the Episcopal Church is the result of a long historical development. It is unfortunate that it is sometimes the occasion of partisan controversy.

The ideal schedule of corporate worship in the Church, as laid out in the Prayer Book, is seldom realized in any of our parishes. This would entail Morning and Evening Prayer daily, including Sundays, frequent use of the Lit-

---

[7] See *Chapters in Church History*, pp. 230-35. It should be noted that in the eighteenth century John Wesley and the early Evangelicals laid much stress upon frequent celebrations of Holy Communion, and also upon adequate preparation.

any, and a celebration of the Holy Communion, with proper preparation for it, at least every Sunday and holy day, not merely as an "extra" service, but as part of the regular corporate life of the whole parish. Such a discipline of worship would not mean necessarily that every lay person would make his or her communion at every celebration. The frequency of reception of communion by the laity is a matter that the Church leaves to each person's need and conscience. What the law of the Church does require is that every member consider it his "bounden duty" to "worship God every Sunday in his Church" (Prayer Book, p. 291).

THE ANTE-COMMUNION [8]

The Prayer Book rite of Holy Communion consists of two parts which were originally independent liturgies. The first part, known as the Ante-Communion, may still be used as an independent service. It is a liturgy built around the reading and preaching of God's Word. Historically, it has had both an educational and a missionary purpose, to bring men to the knowledge of God's redemption in Christ. When used in conjunction with the second part, the Eucharist proper, it serves as a preparation for our participation in the sacrament. Yet there is a sense, too, in which it might be said that the Eucharist is a response of the Church to the saving Gospel that is proclaimed in the Ante-Communion. In any case, the two parts of our rite are complementary one to the other. In both of them we hear and receive God's holy Word.

---

[8] The ancient technical name for Ante-Communion, sometimes used today, is the *Pro-Anaphora,* i.e., the part prior to the "Sacrifice."

The liturgy of Ante-Communion may be outlined as follows (with optional parts placed in brackets):

[Introit—a psalm, hymn, or anthem, or the Litany]
[Lord's Prayer—a survival of the priest's preparation, usually said quietly by the celebrant alone]
The Collect for Purity
The Commandments (either the Ten Commandments or our Lord's Summary of the Law, or both) with the response:
Kyrie eleison ("Lord, have mercy upon us")
[The Prayer, "O Almighty Lord," after the Commandments]
The Salutation and Collect of the Day
The Epistle
[Gradual—a psalm, hymn, or anthem]
The Gospel, with its responses:
   Gloria tibi ("Glory be to thee, O Lord") and *Laus Christe* ("Praise be to thee, O Christ")
The Creed (usually the Nicene Creed, sometimes the Apostles' Creed)
[Prayers]
The Sermon

The distinctively Anglican feature of this liturgy is the introduction of the Commandments.[9] In the Latin Mass, the liturgy opens with resounding paeans of praise. After the Introit Psalm, the *Kyrie eleison* and (on festivals) the *Gloria in excelsis* precede the Salutation and Collect of the Day. The *Kyrie* is not penitential in character, but has its

---

[9] Since the 1928 revision, the American Prayer Book has required that the Ten Commandments be read "at least one Sunday in each month."

ancient flavor as an acclamation of praise to God. Cranmer followed this order closely in the first Prayer Book, but in the second Prayer Book of 1552, he moved the *Gloria* to the end of the service, and turned the *Kyrie* into a penitential response to the Commandments. This is indeed a more somber opening than that of the Latin Mass, even when we use a hymn or psalm of praise for an introit. But the beginning of our liturgy is none the less an impressive one.

The Collect for Purity with which our service formally opens has been called the noblest of all the collects in the Prayer Book. It places us at once in relation to all Three Persons of the Blessed Trinity, reminds us that absolute sincerity is the condition of all true worship, and points us to the proper end of all true worship: love of God and worthy praise of His Name. The prayer is a fitting introduction both to the entire service and, in particular, to the examination of our conscience by the Commandments of God.

The Commandments, whether in the full form of the Ten Commandments or in the Summary of the Law in our Lord's words, confront us with the absolute claim of God upon our lives. There is no escape from it. He made us for Himself, to love Him and to love one another in Him, with everything we are and have. Yet how cold we are in His worship, how neglectful of His honor, how selfish and deceitful in our relations with our neighbors! Surely in His sight can no man justify himself. All we can possibly say is "Lord, have mercy upon us."

Will God have mercy? The answer to this question comes in the next portion of the service, the lessons from

Scripture with their introductory Collect of the Day.[10] In these "propers," which vary from Sunday to Sunday and season to season, God's answer to our need for reconciliation is presented in manifold ways. But all of them turn upon one and the same reply: In God's Son mankind has fulfilled the Law. Through Him mankind has been reconciled to God. The Gospel lesson is thus the climax of Ante-Communion. It is marked out by a special ceremony, our standing to hear it read, and by the responses of "Glory be to thee" and "Praise be to thee" that surround its reading.

There is another mark of honor given to the Gospel, in a ceremony whose significance is seldom understood. It is generally read on the "north" side of the holy Table, or at a lectern or pulpit on the "north" side. In the ancient churches the sanctuary was usually located in the eastern end of the building. The celebrant took his place behind the Table, facing the people and looking toward the west. The place of lesser honor was at his left hand; the place of greater honor at his right. The lessons of lesser honor (there were originally two of them, an Old Testament lesson as well as an Epistle from the New Testament) were therefore read from the south side, while the Gospel lesson was accorded the honor of being read from the right or north side. The movement of the service book from the Epistle to the Gospel side of the holy Table, so commonly witnessed now, is a simple survival of a solemn Gospel procession. This procession, also seen today in many of our churches, accompanied the Gospel Book as it was

---

[10] This section of the service is still marked off from what precedes by the ancient salutation before the Collect: "The Lord be with you," etc.

brought forth to be read at an appointed place. During the procession a psalm-chant or anthem was sung, called the gradual, from the step (*gradus*) of the pulpit from which it was chanted.

Following the Gospel the Church reaffirms its faith in the saving Word by recital of the Creed. The Nicene Creed is usually used, for this Creed is universally acknowledged by the whole Church, East and West, as the great, historic bulwark of its belief that in Christ God Himself became man for our salvation. Then follows the sermon, in which living testimony is given to this Gospel and Creed, and men are called to faith and loving obedience. It is significant that in the Prayer Book sermons are mentioned only in connection with the Holy Communion. They are interpretative links that relate the saving Word of God proclaimed in the lessons to the actions that follow in the eucharistic celebration.

Ante-Communion is a brief liturgy, but it has a tremendous scope. It is nothing less than a summary of the whole drama of our redemption. It takes us all the way from the Law of God proclaimed to Israel at Mount Sinai to the revelation of the Gospel of His Son; and on beyond, through the ages of the historic Church, down to our present day and hour. Yet the focal center around which it all revolves is the Gospel. Our response to this Gospel will now unfold in the eucharistic action proper. For in the Eucharist the Church realizes in its own corporate life the redemption it has won in our Lord Jesus Christ.

THE OFFERTORY

The second part of the Holy Communion has three principal divisions: the Offertory, the Consecration, and the

Communion. These three divisions represent, respectively: the preparation of the holy Table, the giving of thanks over the gifts laid there, and the receiving of the consecrated gifts in fellowship with our Lord and with one another.

The Offertory, or preparation of the Eucharist, may be outlined as follows:

The Offering of our Alms
The Offering of our Oblations of Bread and Wine

(These are accompanied by devotions, such as the Offertory Sentences, and an Offertory hymn or anthem.)

The Offering of our Prayers: for Christ's Church
The Offering of our Penitence:

The Invitation
The Confession
The Absolution
The Comfortable Words

The fourth section of the Offertory, the offering of our penitence, was originally a pre-communion devotion. In the second Prayer Book of 1552 Cranmer placed it immediately before the Consecration. In this Book there was no Offertory of the bread and wine, and Ante-Communion ended with the Prayer for the Church. Thus the penitential devotion served as a preparation for the second half of the rite, the Eucharist proper. By including this section here, as a part of the Offertory, we are following in spirit the original intention of Cranmer's change of its position. In the ensuing comments we shall show how necessary this act of penitence is to the offering of our alms, oblations and prayers.

The essential action of the Offertory is the placing of our gifts of bread and wine upon the altar. In the early Church each communicant brought his own individual gift of these oblations, and each one severally took them up to the holy Table at the offering time. In the Middle Ages, when the people did not communicate frequently, they did not bring these offerings. Hence the priest or his assistant made the offerings for them. In more recent times we have usually had a server act as the representative of the congregation in this action. But in many parishes today something of the ancient custom is being revived, in that representatives of the congregation bring to the celebrant the offerings of bread and wine from the main body of the church, along with the offerings of alms.

No matter how the oblations are prepared and presented, they are outward tokens of *ourselves,* no less than they are signs by which our Lord Himself will come to us. We are bound up in them, because they are the fruit of our labor upon God's creation. They are symbols of our stewardship over all the rich gifts with which God has endowed us. Yet we do not offer God's gifts in the form of wheat and grapes. We have to make them into bread and wine. Hence they testify before God to our use of His property, which He has bestowed upon us, and to the way in which we labor with it for the welfare of one another. The Offertory is therefore a witness for or against our total common life together in all its manifold relationships. It is here that we see most clearly that our religion cannot be divorced from our politics, our economics, and our social and cultural activities.

Every family meal is a parable of our interdependence upon the labor and service of countless numbers of people:

farmers, transport workers, manufacturers, salesmen, miners, silversmiths and embroiderers. The list of persons who make possible even the simplest meal we eat seems almost endless, and it reaches to the far corners of the globe. The Church's family meal, the Eucharist, is no different. Do we know all the people who planted and reaped the wheat, who made it into flour and then into bread, who shipped and marketed it, and delivered it into our hands to place upon God's altar? Similarly, do we know anything about the working conditions of those who gathered and pressed the grapes and made them into wine? Do we care about them?

A remarkable study by the Brazilian scholar Josué de Castro entitled *The Geography of Hunger*[11] has been published for the United Nations. In this book we are informed that two-thirds of the world's population are hungry, and that in recent times more people have died of famine than have been killed in war. Yet the resources of the earth are so rich that, with proper political and economic organization upon an international scale, no one need die for want of bread. How can Christians break bread together in God's house, how can they dare ask God to make this bread for them Christ's Body, unless they are deeply concerned for economic and social justice even "unto one of the least of these"—Christ's brethren? As we do unto them, so we do unto Him.

The judgment of God upon our offerings becomes all the more acute when we think about the alms we bring in association with the bread and wine. It is through the alms that we not only support the work of the Church, but dis-

[11] Boston: Little, Brown and Co., 1952. See also, Stringfellow Barr, *Let's Join the Human Race,* Chicago: University of Chicago Press, 1950.

pense the Church's charity. How do we earn our money? How do we spend it? Is all of it consecrated to the love of God and our neighbor? These questions bring us face to face with greed and waste, exploitation and injustice, racial and class prejudices, contempt of "foreigners," lack of concern about the standard of living of all men for whom Christ died.

Then when we have laid our offerings of alms and oblations upon the altar, we offer our prayers for the whole, i.e., healthy, state of Christ's Church. This prayer is an intercession for the Church and its several members—Christians who bear the responsibility of government, the ministry and our congregations, those who are in sorrow and need, and all our faithful departed brethren. In these intercessions we ask God to accept our gifts, and to do so for certain intentions—above all, for "the spirit of truth, unity and concord . . . that all those who do confess thy holy Name may agree in the truth of thy holy Word, and live in unity and godly love." Truth, unity and peace—there is very little of it in our world. But if we look at the Church itself, we discover that there is far from enough of it among professing Christians. The disunity of the Church, the scandal of partisanship and uncharitableness in our own branch of the Church—these, too, lay us under God's judgment in the Offertory.

The truth of the matter is that we do not and we cannot make an offering that is without the stain of our sin. God cannot accept our offering as it is. And yet He does accept it, because of His infinite love for us for Jesus Christ's sake. This is indeed a great mystery of our redemption. He takes the gifts of His own creation that we have soiled, cleanses them in the pure offering of His only Son, and restores them to us consecrated with His life. Hence we must, at whatever cost, bring our offerings to His altar with the deepest penitence, that we may receive His pardon and forgiveness. "We acknowledge and bewail our manifold sins and wickedness . . . Provoking most justly thy wrath and indignation . . . The remembrance of them is grievous unto us; The burden of them is intolerable." These words, which to many seem so over-wrought, so terrible, can hardly convey what really are the facts. They can never match, even so, the infinite reaches of love extended in the comfortable, i.e., strengthening, Words: "So God loved the world that he gave his only-begotten Son"; "If any man sin, we have an Advocate with the Father, Jesus Christ the righteous; and he is the Propitiation for our sins."

THE CONSECRATION

The Prayer of Consecration is the hymn of thanksgiving that we offer to God for His gifts, and in particular for His supreme Gift. It may be outlined as follows:

The *Sursum corda* ("Lift up your hearts"), with

   Preface (including Proper Prefaces for special days and
       seasons)
   Sanctus ("Holy, Holy, Holy")

The Thanksgiving for our Redemption, including
   The Words of Institution
The Oblation of the gifts, and the Memorial
The Invocation of the Word and Holy Spirit
The Oblation of ourselves, with prayer for the benefits
   of communion, concluding with
   The Doxology and Amen
The Lord's Prayer

The order of this prayer comes to our American Prayer Book from the Scottish communion service. It is more nearly akin to the Consecration Prayer in the first Prayer Book of 1549 than is the present form in the English Prayer Book. But it is also closely modeled on the consecration prayers of the Eastern liturgies of antiquity. Thus our American Prayer of Consecration is directly related to the "thankgiving" of the early Christians at their Eucharists.

The form of our Consecration Prayer is derived from a table grace, such as our Lord used at the Last Supper. The Jews always blessed things, including their food, by thanking God for them. To thank God for a gift means that we recognize it as belonging to Him (for He created all things), and therefore we accept it as a sacred trust. We dare not use it other than according to His will. We have already noted in a preceding chapter[12] how the Jewish table thanksgivings on holy days recalled God's redemption of His people, as well as His provident nourishment of them, and offered a petition for the coming of His Kingdom. Our Consecration Prayer is essentially a translation of these Jewish conceptions into Christian terms. The redeeming action of God that we recall is the sacrifice of our Lord. Our petition is made for the coming of the Holy Spirit to sanctify our gifts, that through them we may be united to our risen, ascended Lord.

The Consecration is as much a hymn as it is a prayer. Both the beginning of it (the *Sursum corda,* Preface and *Sanctus*) and the end of it (the Doxology and Amen)

---

[12] See Chapter IV.

frame it with praise.[13] Through this praise we are lifted to the heavenly places to join with the whole company of heaven in adoration to the Triune God. We are lifted up in heart and mind, also, to intimate union with our Lord, who pleads for us eternally before His Father's throne the benefits of His one "full, perfect, and sufficient sacrifice." Here in these moments heaven and earth become one, and we really anticipate in the present time the ultimate reign of God in His everlasting Kingdom.

Our thanksgiving for our Lord's redemption of us leads inevitably to the recalling of the words and actions with which He gave us the memorial of His sacrifice. Then in the Oblation we offer to God the sacred gifts "in remembrance" of all His redeeming acts. Yet in order for God to accept these gifts He must hallow them. Hence in the Invocation we call upon Him to sanctify them by His Word and Holy Spirit, that so consecrated they may actually be to us the very Body and Blood of our Lord.

In the final paragraph of the prayer we complete our offering by presenting to God (in words reminiscent of Romans 12:1) our whole life, our bodies and our souls, to be a holy sacrifice. And this we plead, not for any merits of our own, but because our Lord takes over our offering and makes it one with His own. Here we penetrate into the deepest mystery of our eucharistic sacrifice. Here Christ and His Church become one, in the complete giving over to God of everything we are and have. Thus "the Church,"

---

[13] Thus in the choral Eucharist the beginning and end of the Consecration are sung. The traditional melody of the *Sursum corda* and Preface (The Hymnal, 1940, No. 734) is the oldest chant used in the Church. It is at least as old as the fourth century, if not more ancient.

said St. Augustine, "since it is the Body of which Christ is the Head, learns to offer itself through Himself." [14]

If ever we are "bold to say" the prayer our Lord taught us, it is now. Now united to Him, we can offer the Lord's Prayer as He would have us offer it. In this context it both sums up the whole purpose of the eucharistic action, and at the same time prepares us to receive communion. For the purpose of this action is nothing less than the coming of God's Kingdom "on earth as it is in heaven." Yet this transcendent goal is brought immediately to bear upon our daily life here and now, our struggle against physical want and spiritual ruin. "Give us this day our daily bread . . . Deliver us from evil." When all men come to do God's will and so share with one another their daily bread, as in the Eucharist the holy Bread is shared, then indeed shall be manifest "the kingdom, and the power, and the glory" of God "for ever and ever."

THE COMMUNION

The service concludes as follows:

The Prayer of Humble Access
[The Communion hymn, or anthem]
The Communion:
    Administration of the Bread
    Administration of the Cup
The Post-Communion Thanksgiving
The *Gloria in excelsis* (or some proper hymn)
The Blessing

The Prayer of Humble Access and the Post-Communion Thanksgiving are peculiar to the Prayer Book. But they

---

[14] *The City of God*, x. 20.

correspond in theme to pre-communion and post-communion devotions in other liturgies. The Post-Communion Thanksgiving, in particular, is a most remarkable summary of the whole doctrine of the Eucharist. As noted above, the *Gloria in excelsis* was moved by Cranmer to this place in the 1552 Book, to serve as part of our post-communion thanksgiving. By long established custom we do not normally use it in penitential seasons, but in place of it substitute a "proper" hymn, i.e., a doxology-hymn of praise, or a hymn proper to the season. The ancient Blessing is prefaced in our Prayer Book by an apt citation of Philippians 4:7.

With communion the whole Eucharistic drama reaches its fulfillment. For the purpose of all sacrifice is that we may be united to God. "True sacrifice," to quote St. Augustine again, "is every work which is done that we may be united to God in holy society, and which has a reference to that supreme good and end in which alone we can be truly blessed." [15] Such a union is possible for us because our Lord, who is one with His Father, is also one with us. "We receive what we are, and we are what we receive," said St. Augustine in one of his sermons.

But communion involves also our union one with another. "We are very members incorporate in the mystical body of thy Son, which is the blessed company of all faithful people." The piece of bread and the drop of wine that were offered for me is shared by another; and his offering is in turn part of my communion. Our separate offerings were made one, and blessed as one. When they are returned to us, as we kneel and receive them individually, their unity is not broken. For though the bread is broken

---

[15] *Ibid.*, x., 6.

that each may have a piece, the whole Christ is bestowed in every fragment. "So we, being many, are one body in Christ, and every one members one of another" (Romans 12:5).

The communion devotions remind us of another very important truth. The sacrament is received to the health and preservation of our bodies as well as of our souls. It cleanses and empowers the whole of life. Communion does not take us out of the realm of the physical and material. It does not divorce us from the workaday world in which our daily efforts are mainly spent. Indeed it sends us forth to it to do "all such good works as [God] has prepared for us to walk in." There is no impenetrable wall between the sanctuary and the street. We have already seen how the life we lead in home, and farm, and office, and factory, is wrapped up in the bread and wine we offer. This life is not removed when Christ comes to fill these gifts. It is redeemed and given back. And it is given back with the promise and the power of a better offering at the next Eucharist.

THE OBLIGATION OF THE EUCHARIST

The Holy Communion witnesses to the central affirmations of our Christian faith. It is a "Gospel" sacrament in the fullest sense. "As often as ye eat this bread, and drink this cup," said St. Paul, "ye do shew the Lord's death till he come" (I Cor. 11:26). By this rite we proclaim to ourselves and to the world the saving purpose and action of God. The Holy Communion exhibits also, as does no other activity of the Church, the true nature and promise of Christian fellowship, of a society patterned after God's will. For it brings us a foretaste of the final consummation of all the ages, when Christ is acknowledged by every creature as Lord. The Church cannot exist without it. For it is essential to its life, both to express it and to renew it.

Throughout the ages countless men and women have risked their lives and fortunes to meet together for the Eucharist. Many have given up life itself lest they neglect it or betray it. Such were those martyrs of the now-forgotten town of ancient North Africa, whose testimony was introduced at the beginning of this book. These people did not meet together for the mere thrill of dangerous adventure. Certainly it was not because of sheer obstinacy or habit. They risked their lives because this was the way, ultimately the only way, they could realize that which they were called and redeemed of God to be—members one of another in Jesus Christ.

To be a Christian it is not enough to have kindly thoughts and words and deeds. It is not enough to have right beliefs about God. It is not even enough to pour out the heart continually in prayer and thanksgiving. These things are rather the fruit of a far more basic obligation. We must be reconciled, reconciled to God and to one another. Even as our Lord surrendered, gave over and offered His entire life to His Father's will and love, so must His disciples give over in sacrifice themselves, their souls and bodies, to Him and to one another in Him. For this "bounden duty and service" no man is sufficient of himself. He must fulfill it in Holy Communion. "Except ye eat the flesh of the Son of man, and drink his blood, ye have no life in you" (John 6:53).

Christian Initiation: Baptism, Instruction and Confirmation

WE ENTER the Church by a process of initiation that establishes a unique relationship to God for all time and for all eternity. We join a society to whose faith we give our allegiance and to whose rules we promise obedience. Yet initiation into the Church is far more than a voluntary joining of a society of like-minded people. In fact, we do not join the Church so much as we are joined into it. In our Christian initiation it is God who takes the initiative. The Church is His family and "household of faith." Though all men are children of God, in our initiation into His Church we become so in a unique way. By His gracious act He adopts us into that family as sons and heirs, joint-heirs with His Son Jesus Christ. By His free gift we are "born anew" and made living members of His family by the Holy Spirit that He imparts. And to those who remain faithful in this relationship He pledges an inheritance that is nothing less than eternal life.

A Christian so initiated may at some later time, of

course, break his promises or neglect to fulfill them. He may even deny his Christian name. But he can never break or give back or exchange the mark of his family relationship. A wayward son is still a son. His birth in the family of God can never be undone, never repeated. It is, in truth, an "everlasting benediction." Hence the initial question at the opening of the baptismal service ("Hath this Person been already baptized, or no?") reminds us of a once-for-all act of God's redeeming love and grace.

The initiatory liturgy of the Prayer Book consists of three parts: the Ministration of Holy Baptism, the Offices of Instruction, and the Order of Confirmation or Laying on of Hands. In the case of children who are baptized in infancy the initiation follows this order or sequence, and is completed only after the baptized child has reached the age of discretion. Adult converts to the Christian faith and fellowship, who were not baptized in childhood, are given their instruction before Baptism; and they are confirmed as soon after their Baptism as possible, sometimes at the same service. In such cases the initiation is comparable to the practice of the ancient Church, when Baptism and Confirmation were normally administered together. How and why Baptism and Confirmation came to be separated we shall discuss in a later section of this chapter. Meanwhile we should give some consideration to the origin of our rites of Christian initiation, both in their institution by our Lord and in their observance by the Church in apostolic times.

ORIGINS OF CHRISTIAN INITIATION

The ceremony of a baptism, or washing with water, was very common in the religions of antiquity, where it generally symbolized a spiritual cleansing. Such purifications prepared the initiate for intimate communion with the divine or for fellowship with a religious community. Among the Jews, for example, a baptism was administered to proselytes from the Gentile world. It cleansed them from the stains of heathenism and made them fit to be joined with the chosen people of God. It was said by one of the rabbis that a proselyte coming forth from baptism was like a newborn child. Children born to a proselyte after his baptism were counted "clean," while those born before his baptism were "unclean" unless they also were initiated.

To what extent the practice of proselyte baptism among the Jews influenced the development of the Church's initiation is not certainly known. But there can be no question about the importance, for Christian practice, of the rite of John the Baptist. John was a preacher of righteousness, a prophet of an impending judgment of God upon men for their sin. He called both Jews and Gentiles to repentance and earnest preparation for the coming of God's Kingdom. Those who responded to his summons he baptized, as a sign and sacrament of their inward conversion and hope of salvation in the coming Day of Judgment. They literally passed through the waters of Jordan, as their fathers had done with Joshua of old, into the land of promise, the kingdom promised of God.

Our Lord Himself received baptism at John's hands. As He came up from the baptismal waters the Holy Spirit descended upon Him, and He became fully conscious of His unique relationship with His Father and of the divine purpose of His coming upon earth. He knew Himself to be the Messiah, the Son of God, sent to bring His Father's

Kingdom.[1] It is no exaggeration to say that the Baptism of Jesus became for the Church the very basis and example of its own rite of initiation. Those who would become one with His Body must undergo, as He did, a baptism in water for the forgiveness of sin, and be endowed with His Spirit for a new life of service to their heavenly King. Hence from its very beginning, on that famous day of Pentecost, the Church has summoned men to: "Repent, and be baptized every one of you in the name of Jesus Christ for the remission of sins, and ye shall receive the gift of the Holy Ghost" (Acts 2:38).

Whether our Lord expressly commanded His disciples to practice Baptism is a subject much debated by Biblical scholars. The classic texts referring to His institution of Baptism are: 1) the Great Commission in Matthew 28:19: "Go ye therefore, and teach all nations, baptizing them in the name of the Father, and of the Son, and of the Holy Ghost"; and 2) His remark to Nicodemus, recorded in John 3:5: "Except a man be born of water and of the Spirit, he cannot enter into the kingdom of God." They testify in any case to the belief of first-century Christians that Jesus had given specific direction to His Church to baptize those who believe in Him.[2]

At one point in His ministry our Lord referred to His death as a baptism (see Mark 10:38 f.), a baptism which His disciples also must undergo if they would share His future glory in His Father's Kingdom. He did not mean that all His followers must be literally martyrs, baptized in blood, but that they must all be prepared to be so. That

---

[1] See *The Holy Scriptures*, pp. 130-31.
[2] One may refer to the commentaries on Matthew and John listed in the bibliography in *The Holy Scriptures*, pp. 212-13.

is to say, we must be so joined to Him that we are truly dead to the world of sin and alive with Him "in newness of life." The death and Resurrection of our Lord are shared by us in Baptism, as St. Paul so clearly saw:

Know ye not, that so many of us as were baptized into Jesus Christ were baptized into his death? Therefore we are buried with him by baptism into death: that like as Christ was raised up from the dead by the glory of the Father, even so we also should walk in newness of life. For if we have been planted together in the likeness of his death, we shall be also in the likeness of his resurrection: Knowing this, that our old man is crucified with him, that the body of sin might be destroyed, that henceforth we should not serve sin. (Romans 6:3-6.)

IN THE EARLY CHURCH

The Book of Acts and the Epistles of the New Testament tell us more about the meaning of Christian initiation than they do about the details of its ministration. Its gifts of grace included: forgiveness of sin, spiritual regeneration (i.e., rebirth),[3] the indwelling presence of the Holy Spirit, incorporation into the Church with all its privileges, and a promise of eternal life. The following points may serve to summarize the way in which these gifts of grace were imparted:

1. *Preparation for Baptism.* Repentance and faith in Christ were demanded of all candidates for Baptism. Instruction was given according to the needs and religious backgrounds of the candidates. In the earlier days, when most of the converts were Jews, instruction was confined largely to proofs from the Scriptures that Jesus was the

---

[3] Regeneration must not be confused with conversion. Regeneration is the act of God in establishing a new relationship between us and Himself. Conversion is a change in our own attitude towards that relationship.

Messiah of God. When the Church became predominantly Gentile, a longer and more systematic period of instruction was necessary, both for teaching the Christian faith and also for discipline in Christian morals. Exercises of prayer and fasting were enjoined. By the end of the second century the period of training before Baptism was normally three years. Intensive instruction and devotional exercises took place during the fast before Easter, when Baptism normally came to be administered. (See Chapter V.)

2. *The Mode of Baptism.* Baptism in water was customarily by immersion, for the Greek word "baptize" literally means "to dip." The immersion might be done in running streams or in pools, where such a supply of water was available. An early second century document, the Didache, directs the baptizer to "pour water on the head" if there is not a sufficient amount of water at hand for immersion. The oldest pictures of Christian Baptism (late second century) portray the candidate standing up to his knees in a stream or pool, while the one baptizing pours water over the head so that the whole body is washed. The Eastern Church still uses immersion in Baptism. Our Prayer Book also keeps the ancient custom in mind, in the rubric (p. 279) that directs the minister (". . . he shall dip him in the Water discreetly, or shall pour Water upon him").

3. *The Name of God.* Ancient peoples, both Jews and pagans, had a profound reverence for the divine power released when a sacred name was invoked. To invoke it in vain was the utmost blasphemy. To say the Name of God over a person or a thing was to bring it into the possession of God and under His subjection. It identified the person

or object as belonging to Him. Thus in Christian Baptism the naming of God over the baptized signifies a relationship therein established. The initiate is henceforth, personally and eternally, subject to that Name which is above every name. Though there is some evidence that in the earliest days Baptism was administered in the Name of Jesus only, the use of the Triune Name is certainly as old as the apostolic age. Ever since that time the Church has considered the naming of all three Persons of the Blessed Trinity as absolutely necessary for a valid Baptism. It is in the faith of this God that we are pledged; and it is in the Name of this God that we are redeemed for an eternal inheritance.

4. *The Laying on of Hands.* The New Testament documents are not always very clear, or even consistent, in what they tell us of the gift of the Spirit in the initiation rite. Sometimes the Spirit is imparted before the Baptism (Acts 10:44 f.), sometimes immediately after (Acts 19:5-6). In other cases there was an interval of time between the Baptism and the giving of the Spirit by the laying on of hands (Acts 8:14 ff.). Whether the laying on of hands always accompanied Baptism as the means of giving the Spirit is not certain, but it is more than likely that this was the case. The ceremony of laying on of hands was a familiar one in Judaism, for the imparting of a special blessing or commission. There are, however, some passages in the Epistles that have been taken as referring to an "anointing" in connection with the gift of the Spirit.[4]

5. *The Chrism.* The ancients customarily anointed themselves with oil or ointments when bathing, much as we use soap and fragrant perfumes. It would not be un-

---

[4] See especially II Cor. 1:21-22, Eph. 1:13-14, 4:30, and I John 2:20.

usual, therefore, if such a custom had obtained from earliest times in connection with the "bath" of Baptism. It is easy to see, too, how symbolic meanings could be associated with it. The word Messiah (in Greek, *Christos*) means "anointed One." In the Old Testament, rites of anointing were associated with the consecration of kings and priests. But Christ is the Christian's anointed King and Priest, and those initiated into His Body must therefore share in His Kingship and Priesthood. Thus, as time went on, the rich symbolism of anointing came to overshadow in importance the basic ceremony of the laying on of hands. In both the Eastern Orthodox and the Roman Catholic Churches, the blessed oil for anointing, called *chrism,* came to be viewed as the essential element in Confirmation. Yet there is no good authority for taking the references in the New Testament Epistles to our "anointing" with the Holy Spirit as anything other than a vivid figure of speech.[5] The use of "chrism" is not so apostolic as the laying on of hands. The Prayer Book usage is nearer to the original custom than are the "anointings" of the Roman and Orthodox Communions.

6. *The Minister of the Sacrament.* The right to baptize has never been restricted to any order of the ministry. Any Christian may baptize, but in the normal course of things, since Baptism is a public liturgy of the Church, it will be administered by the Church's ordained ministers. In the Book of Acts, however, the gift of the Spirit through the laying on of hands is usually associated with the apostles. There is only one exception—the initiation of St. Paul by Ananias (9:17). It is possible, however, that in this in-

---

[5] See G. W. H. Lampe, *The Seal of the Spirit,* London: Longmans, Green and Co., 1951, pp. 3-18.

stance we are dealing not with a "Confirmation" but with an act of healing. In any event, the Church after New Testament times restricted the laying on of hands in initiation to the bishop, who was viewed as the successor of the apostles. The bishop usually presided over the entire initiation liturgy, though he did not actually perform the baptisms. But immediately after the candidates had been baptized he laid his hands upon them and anointed them with the chrism. In the Western Church, Roman and Anglican, the bishop is still the minister of confirmation. But in the Eastern Churches, the priest is allowed to confirm, provided he use chrism that has been blessed by the bishop.

INFANT BAPTISM

No subject connected with Christian initiation has been more keenly debated than the propriety of infant Baptism. Certain Christian bodies absolutely refuse to baptize any child who has not reached the age of discretion on the grounds that: 1) such a practice has no warrant in the New Testament, and 2) the conscious profession of faith and allegiance by the one being baptized is necessary to the validity of the sacrament. On the contrary, those Churches which do practice infant Baptism (and these represent the vast majority of Christians) argue that: 1) infant Baptism is consonant with the teaching and practice of New Testament times, and 2) since the grace of Baptism is a free gift of God, and not a reward for a man's faith, it is certainly God's pleasure that infants be brought within the relationship of God's family, the Church.

It is true that there is no specific mention of the baptism of infants in the New Testament, though it may be implied in the several references to the baptism of "households." [6] In Judaism an infant male was "sealed" into the covenant of God's people by circumcision. It would have been strange indeed if Christian parents had not desired that their children have a share in the grace of the new covenant. For the Lord Himself, during His earthly ministry, had taken children into His arms and blessed them, and had said to His disciples, "Suffer the little children to come unto me, and forbid them not: for of such is the kingdom of God" (Mark 10:13 ff.). That Baptism was viewed as taking the place of circumcision was expressly stated by St. Paul when he described Baptism as "the circumcision made without hands" (Col. 2:10 ff.).

There is enough evidence from Christian writings of the second century to indicate that infant Baptism was practiced by that time and that it was not considered to be a recent innovation. However, so long as the Church was a missionary society in a predominantly heathen world, adult Baptism was of necessity the normal practice, and infant Baptism an exception. The same condition holds true in many missionary areas today. Only when the number of Christians exceeded the pagan population, and Christian influences permeated all areas of ancient society, did infant Baptism become the more customary usage. The development of infant Baptism was particularly strengthened in the fifth century as a result of the controversy of St. Augustine with the heretic Pelagius.[7] Inasmuch as Pelagius denied that man was a fallen creature he contended that we are not born with "original sin." Though he did not reject the custom of infant Baptism, he maintained

---

[6] Acts 16:15, 33 (cf. also 10:47); I Cor. 1:16.
[7] See *Chapters in Church History,* pp. 58, 95-96.

that in the Baptism of infants there was no remission of sin. St. Augustine went to the other extreme in his position; namely, that an unbaptized infant cannot be saved because he has not received God's forgiveness for the sin of Adam. But he was certainly right in insisting upon the fact that all men are sinners in their fallen nature, and that in Baptism both infants and adults receive God's forgiveness.[8] In any event, the influence of St. Augustine's teaching had much to do with the enhancement of infant Baptism. Since his time it has become the normal usage of the Church.

To deny Baptism to infants is to deny the primary truth of what is effected by Baptism. For in Baptism it is not man who takes the initiative, but God. God adopts us as His children, and gives us freely the benefits of our Lord's redeeming work. He places us in a relationship to Him and to His Church whereby we are enabled to resist "the temptations of the world, the flesh, and the devil," and to grow up in all things after His likeness. By Baptism we are "strengthened with might by his Spirit in the inner man; that, Christ dwelling in [our] hearts by faith, [we] may be filled with all the fulness of God." [9] Our nature is changed, by an act of spiritual rebirth. And this act— what we call "regeneration"—only God can accomplish. No man can ever earn it or merit it, no matter how willing and ready he may be for it in both heart and mind. We are "accepted" by God into His family, before we "accept" our new status and relationship.

Yet it is important also that we accept this inheritance

---

[8] On "original sin," see *The Faith of the Church*, pp. 63-65. Our Church does *not* teach the doctrine of the damnation of unbaptized infants.

[9] From the blessing at the conclusion of the Baptismal service, Prayer Book, p. 281. Cf. Eph. 3:16-19.

and all the blessings that it brings. There must come a time when we consciously take it upon our own responsibility. What our parents or sponsors accepted in our name at our Baptism should also be ours by our own deliberate choice. Only thus can we rightfully share in the highest privileges of our membership in God's family, or claim to the full the promises made to us. In this sense Confirmation is the completion of our initiation into God's family. In Baptism we are made members of it indeed; but in Confirmation we become responsible for our membership. Yet even in Confirmation we are recipients of God's gifts of grace, by the imparting of His Holy Spirit to strengthen us and help us in our responsibilities.

THE SEPARATION OF BAPTISM
AND CONFIRMATION

In the early Church Baptism and Confirmation were generally administered in a single service, usually at the Easter Even rites.[10] Occasionally, when there was imminent danger of death, a candidate for Christian initiation was baptized privately. If he survived the crisis he was at a later time confirmed by the bishop. With the rapid growth of the Church after the time of Constantine, and particularly with the increasing custom of infant Baptism, the bishops delegated to parish priests the right to baptize at any time. In the Eastern Church, the priests were also allowed to confirm, provided they used chrism blessed by the bishop. But in the West, the Church in Rome forbade the ministration of Confirmation except by the Bishop, and its practice of separating Baptism and

---

[10] See Chapter IV for a description of Christian initiation about the year 200, as related by St. Hippolytus.

Confirmation into two distinct rites was followed wherever the Roman liturgy was in use.

This separation of initiation into two parts created some confusion with respect to the meaning of Confirmation. The medieval theologians rightly understood that Baptism alone was all that was necessary to make a man a Christian, a member of the Body of Christ. Not only did it convey the forgiveness of sin and spiritual rebirth, but it also imparted the Holy Spirit and the promise of eternal life. Confirmation, on the other hand, was not necessary for a man's salvation, though it was a "sacrament" much to be desired. For in Confirmation an added gift of the Holy Spirit was imparted for "strength," equipping the Christian for witness and combat for his faith.

The English Reformers of the sixteenth century continued the traditional practice of the Western Church, and with it much of the medieval interpretation of the relation of Baptism and Confirmation. In the Prayer Book, Baptism is referred to as regeneration with the Holy Spirit and incorporation into Christ's Church; Confirmation is a strengthening and increase of the Holy Spirit to those already regenerated "by Water and the Holy Ghost." The Articles of Religion state that Baptism is a sacrament ordained by Christ. But Confirmation is "not to be counted" as a sacrament of the Gospel comparable to Baptism and the Lord's Supper. (See Article XXV of the Prayer Book, p. 607.) The English Reformers also kept the tradition that Confirmation is administered only by the Bishop, as the successor of the apostles.

A very significant addition to the Confirmation rite was made, however. Following the lead of Luther, Cranmer prefaced the service with a Catechism, or instruction, which children were to learn before being brought to the bishop for the laying on of hands. Thus he made clear that Confirmation—and with it, admission to the Holy Communion—was not to be administered except to those who had reached an age when they could responsibly take for themselves their baptismal vows. This addition to the Confirmation rite marked a great improvement over medieval practice. During the Middle Ages Confirmation was conferred at any age. No previous instruction was required; nor was it related to admission to the Holy Communion. The Prayer Book, in providing for instruction and a reaffirmation of baptismal vows in connection with Confirmation, recovered a very important element in Christian initiation. It makes certain that in the process of initiation into Christ's Body each individual respond for himself, upon his own responsibility, to the redeeming action of God. Until this response is made, the initiate is not admitted to the highest privileges of the Church's fellowship, in particular, the Holy Communion.

We now turn to a brief consideration of the Prayer Book Offices of initiation:

HOLY BAPTISM

According to the Prayer Book, the rite of Baptism is always administered publicly in the church, except for "urgent cause," preferably at the regular services of the parish on Sundays and Holy Days. Thus the people of God are present not only to receive the new member, but also by their prayers and faith to support and sustain him in his vows. Baptism is not a private liturgy. It is the concern of the whole Body of faithful people. Even when necessity requires the baptism to be administered apart from the Church's regular assembly, there should be "witnesses" to represent the Church.

In the case of infants who are baptized, the promises of faith and obedience are taken in the child's name by Sponsors, or Godparents. (In our American Church, parents are also allowed to serve as Sponsors; for in the "frontier" conditions of early American society it was not always possible for Church families to find suitable Sponsors who lived near them.) Originally, Sponsors were persons who offered a guarantee to the Church that the candidates for Baptism were sincere seekers of membership in the Church. After the age of persecution, however, they became sureties for the Christian nurture and upbringing of the baptized. Sponsors are representatives of the Church who are pledged to a very sacred duty. Much care therefore should be taken in their selection, for the vows they promise both for their godchildren and for themselves are of the utmost importance. The whole Church, too, has an obligation to assist the Sponsors in carrying out their vows, by providing the best opportunities possible for Christian education. In a very true sense, the entire Church is the "sponsor" in Baptism. Individual Sponsors are the Church's spokesmen and agents.

The baptismal service in the Prayer Book consists of five parts:

1. *The Preparation.* The lengthy preparatory rites which were observed in the early Church during the season of Lent are now reduced to a brief summary: a bidding, stating the meaning of Baptism; a prayer invoking God's aid and help to the one to be baptized; a lesson from the Gospels, giving the basis of Baptism in the teaching of our Lord; and a concluding prayer of thanksgiving

for God's gift, and of petition for those now presented to receive it.

2. *The Promises.* The substance of these promises goes back to the earliest times of the Church. The candidate for Baptism vows, either for himself or through his Sponsors, a renunciation of all evil, and pledges his belief in the Christian Faith, as it is summarized in the Apostles' Creed.[11] He promises also to keep the commandments of God. Sponsors for infants promise, in addition, to teach their godchildren the Creed, the Lord's Prayer, and the Ten Commandments, "and all other things which a Christian ought to know and believe to his soul's health." And they engage to bring their godchildren, when sufficiently instructed, to be confirmed by the bishop. Penitence, faith, obedience—these are our human response, God helping us, to God's gracious gifts. A series of brief supplications concludes this part of the service. Originally, these supplications formed part of the following section of the rite:

3. *The Blessing of the Water.* A solemn prayer of thanksgiving and consecration, beginning with the *Sursum corda* ("Lift up your hearts") is now offered over the water that has been poured into the font. In thanksgiving for our redemption and in obedience to our Lord's teaching, we ask God in this prayer to bless the water of Baptism. It is set aside for a sacred use, to be a sign to us of an inward ("mystical") cleansing and spiritual gift of grace.

4. *The Baptism.* At this point we reach the climax of the rite. First of all, the candidate is given a name, his Christian name. By this name he will be known as the

---

[11] For the origin of the Creed, see *Chapters in Church History*, pp. 33-36.

child of God. By this name he will be known and remembered in the prayers of the Church. His name will always be a reminder of the most sacred relationships of his life. With this Christian name the candidate is now baptized in the water, either by immersion or by pouring the water on his head. As God's Name is said over his name, he thereby becomes the eternal possession of the Blessed Trinity. A further ceremony after the Baptism—the signing of the candidate's forehead with the Cross—brings out in a vivid and dramatic way what this discipleship in "Christ's flock" means. "Whosoever will come after me," said Jesus, "let him deny himself, and take up his cross, and follow me" (Mark 8:34). The Cross of Christ is the banner of our warfare "against sin, the world, and the devil," the weapon of our fight, and the crown of our victory.

5. *The Thanksgiving.* It is particularly fitting that the first prayer that the newly baptized says with the Church is the Lord's Prayer. The service then concludes with prayers of thanksgiving and of blessing. In these brief forms the whole wealth of meaning of the baptismal act is summarized: rebirth with the Holy Spirit, incorporation into the Church, death and resurrection with Christ, and the promise of eternal life in the Kingdom of God.

OFFICES OF INSTRUCTION

The Offices of Instruction are a basic guide to the Church's teaching. They are set in the form of worship, for we learn best when our hearts are open to God in praise and prayer. The materials of the offices are drawn for the most part from the Catechism (Prayer Book, pp. 577-83), and cover in a succinct way all those "things which a Christian ought to know and believe to his soul's health."

The first Office of Instruction introduces us to the Creed, the Ten Commandments, and the Lord's Prayer. We are prepared by it for an understanding of the Church's Faith, its ethical standards, and its common worship. These three things have always been essential elements in the training of initiates to Christianity. The second Office of Instruction develops these basic materials with respect to three subjects: the Church, the Sacraments, and the Ministry.

There is no intention on the part of the Church to restrict the instruction of candidates for Baptism and Confirmation either to the content or to the method of these offices. There are indeed many other important subjects, not treated in them, such as the Bible or Church history. There are other methods besides question-and-answer for imparting religious knowledge and experience. The offices are merely a syllabus of fundamentals. Nor should it be overlooked that the offices are designed not solely for children or candidates for initiation, but for the whole Church. We never "graduate" from the Church's schooling. Throughout our lives we are always finding that there is more to learn about the Church's teaching, and new insights to be gained by fresh attention to the fundamentals of its faith, its ethic, and its prayer. A discerning writer has noted that we are directed not to "send" but to "bring" our children and others to instruction, and hence to stay and participate with them in these teaching offices.[12]

---

[12] See E. L. Parsons and B. H. Jones, *The American Prayer Book, Its Origins and Principles*. New York: Charles Scribner's Sons, 1937, p. 241.

THE ORDER OF CONFIRMATION

Confirmation, like Baptism, is a public service of the Church, and only in exceptional cases is it administered "privately." Indeed the visit of the bishop for Confirmation is a significant event in the life of a parish. For the bishop, by virtue of his apostolic office,[13] is a symbol of that wider fellowship and communion of saints in time and place, of which each parish is a part. He represents the whole Church, at the same time that he serves as the chief priest and pastor of the several congregations in his diocese. Thus his participation in the concluding ceremony of the Church's initiation gives to it the widest association. It reminds us that we are members not only of a church, but more importantly of the Church. We do not join a parish church on such and such a street in one particular place or community, nor even the Episcopal Church. We are joined into the Holy Catholic Church of all the ages throughout the whole wide world.

The rite of Confirmation has two parts. In the first section, after the candidates are presented to the bishop and a lesson from the Book of Acts is read, the *candidates* confirm publicly before the congregation their baptismal promises. The second section, beginning with the versicle, "Our help is in the Name of the Lord," is the part in which *God* confirms the candidates with the strengthening gifts of the Holy Spirit through the prayers and laying on of hands by the bishop. Immediately after the laying on of hands, all join in the Lord's Prayer, and the bishop concludes with prayers for the candidates and all the people, and a Blessing.

---

[13] See Chapter X.

In the bishop's prayer before the laying on of hands ("Almighty and everliving God") the Spirit's gifts are listed as sevenfold: wisdom, understanding, counsel, ghostly (i.e., spiritual) strength, knowledge, godliness and holy fear (i.e., reverence and awe). This list is a traditional one, based upon Isaiah's prophecy of the spiritual endowments that would direct and guide the Messiah in the coming Age of God's Kingdom.[14] By our union with our Lord we share in His spiritual gifts, and His Spirit, working inwardly in us, brings our lives more and more into harmony and conformity with His character. The sevenfold gifts of the Spirit are not to be viewed as a set of moral virtues, suddenly implanted in us. They are the influences of a personal relationship which help us to acquire moral virtues and to lead a life holy and acceptable unto God. The Holy Spirit teaches us right principles and assists us in making wise judgments. But more than that, He gives us the strength of will to act upon these principles and judgments and to carry through with their accomplishment in righteous deeds.[15]

With Confirmation we are fully equipped to take our part, responsibly and perseveringly, in whatever service God calls us to bear—to "stand fast in one spirit, with one mind, striving together for the faith of the gospel" (Phil. 1:27). Yet, in truth, Confirmation is not merely the end of a process of initiation but also the beginning of new adventures for God and His Church. His gifts do not end with Confirmation. For now we are privileged

---

[14] Isaiah 11:2. The "sevenfold" list comes from the Greek version of the Old Testament (the Septuagint); in the Hebrew version there are only six.

[15] See *The Faith of the Church*, Chapter VIII.

to share to the fullest extent all the manifold means of His grace given to those who continue steadfastly "in the apostles' doctrine and fellowship, and in breaking of bread, and in prayers" (Acts 2:42).

CHAPTER NINE

"Other Rites and Ceremonies"

THROUGHOUT the course of our daily lives there come times of momentous decision or crisis when we need particular help and assistance from God. The Church's liturgy provides a means whereby such occasions may be hallowed by relating them to God's love and purpose and to the care and concern of His faithful people. Among the most common of these experiences are marriage, childbirth, sickness and death. For each of these occasions the Prayer Book brings to us the blessing of God and the prayer of the Church.

HOLY MATRIMONY

The marriage service has a twofold purpose: 1) In the first place, the Church acts as a witness to a contract in which a man and a woman pledge to each other a life-long union of fidelity and love. Such a vow, made "till death us do part," requires for its fulfillment the highest gifts of grace: love and honor, faithfulness and patience, wisdom and godliness. Where these are present in the marital bond, creating a family whose home is in truth "a haven of blessing and of peace," there is a sacramental sign of that love and union which is "betwixt Christ and his Church." 2) Hence the marriage liturgy of the Church also brings to the wedding vows a blessing of God upon them. The service is not only a witness to a covenant, but also a benediction.

The rite begins with a solemn exhortation, stating the dignity and sacredness of the marital relation, and giving warning both to the assembled congregation and to the couple that the marriage must be lawful, not only according to the civil law but also "as God's Word doth allow." For the minister who solemnizes the marriage acts in a dual capacity. He is both a magistrate, authorized by the civil authority to preside over the marriage vows, and a priest responsible to God and to the Church. He can only bless those parties to Holy Matrimony who engage themselves with sincere intention to fulfill, not only the civil law of the State, but also the divine law of God's Word with respect to the binding force of a life-long vow.

If there is no evidence presented to question the lawfulness of the marriage, the couple then proceed to exchange with each other their promises. The first pair of vows is a final, formal ratification of their engagement. Then the father or guardian of the bride gives her over into the loving care of her groom. The wedding vows are now given, as each party pledges to the other their troth (i.e., fidelity) "from this day forward . . . till death us do part." In token of this pledge a wedding ring is blessed, and given by the man to the woman. The ring was originally a symbol of the dowry, but it now carries a more spiritual meaning, a sign of God's peace and favor.[1]

Prayers are then offered, beginning with the Lord's Prayer. God's blessing is sought for the faithfulness of the couple, the gift of children, and the formation of a Christian home. As he reads the words of our Lord in the

---

[1] Today it is common also for the bride to give a ring to her partner.

gospel (Matt. 19:6) the priest joins the hands of the couple and forthwith declares that they are Man and Wife. The Service concludes with a final benediction.

In addition to the marriage service proper, the Prayer Book provides a special Collect, Epistle and Gospel for the celebration of a Nuptial Eucharist (pp. 267-68). This is in fact the most ancient liturgy of the Church at weddings. For in the earliest days of the Church all marriages were performed before civil magistrates. The Church's blessing consisted only of the nuptial celebration of Holy Communion. Not until relatively late in the Middle Ages did it become customary for a priest to preside over the giving of the marriage vows. Certainly in a covenant that signifies to us "the mystical union that is betwixt Christ and his Church," it is most appropriate that it be sealed at the very beginning with participation in the Eucharist. The fidelity and love that unite Christ and His Church in this Sacrament strengthen and enhance all other bonds of self-giving devotion that we pledge one to another.

A wedding is a sacred occasion. The happy festivity that is appropriate to it should not obscure the fact that the most solemn vows of self-sacrificing love are taken in "the sight of God." The ceremony may be very elaborate or very simple. But in either case it should not be made the occasion for worldly display or entertainment. A sense of reverence, dignity and decency should pervade the service from beginning to end. In particular, when there is music, whether instrumental or vocal or both, it should be selected with a view to its harmony with the words of the rite, the teaching of the Church, and the spiritual profit of those who are present. Popular music, of a sentimental and romantic character, is not suitable to a religious ceremony; in fact, it is contrary to the law of the Church. Only hymns and anthems whose words are taken from the Bible, the Prayer Book or the Church's Hymnal can properly be sung in connection with the Church's liturgical rites (Prayer Book, p. viii). Yet even with this rule, the utmost care should be taken that the music accompanying the words be chosen with discrimination and good taste.[2]

THE CHURCHING OF WOMEN

The brief office of psalmody and prayer for The Thanksgiving of Women after Child-birth—or more commonly, The Churching of Women—is seldom used nowadays. The principal prayer of the rite, however, is often read at other services, such as the Daily Offices or the Holy Communion. The service has a very ancient pedigree; for it goes back to pre-Christian times, to the ceremonial law of the Jews (Lev. 12). The original point of the rite was a "purification" of a woman forty days after childbirth. Thus our Lord's mother observed the custom of the old Law (Luke 2:22 ff.; see Prayer Book, pp. 232-233). Such ideas of a temporary defilement occasioned by childbirth are contrary to Christian teaching. And we owe it to Pope Gregory the Great (590-604) that the office was transformed from one of purification to a service of thanksgiving for a mother's safe preservation "through the great pain and peril of child-birth."

The service may be much enhanced if it includes also a thanksgiving for the gift of children, and associates both parents with the thanksgiving. (At one time the Office

---

[2] See *Music for Church Weddings* (and also *Music for Church Funerals*), by the Joint Commission on Church Music, Greenwich: Seabury Press, 1952.

did include Psalm 127, which speaks of children as "an heritage and gift that cometh of the Lord.") Note that the final rubrics of the Office relate the woman's thanksgiving to offerings for charitable purposes, and also to her participation in the Holy Communion. Thus the personal and individual thanksgiving is taken up into the corporate eucharistic devotion of the whole Church.

VISITATION AND COMMUNION OF THE SICK

The gospels tell us that a large part of our Lord's earthly ministry was devoted to the healing of the sick. He shared the view of His contemporaries that much illness, whether of body or of mind, was the result of demonic spirits. Hence His work of healing was both spiritual and physical in character. At times the health of the body could be restored only after penitence and forgiveness. Yet our Lord did not always attribute illness to sin. In His discrimination of the causes of sickness He had hold of truths which today the medical profession is coming to appreciate more and more. Both the spirit and the body of man are so intimately related that disease, neglect, or even injury, of the one disturbs the order of the other. Thus the ministry of healing in our Lord's Church is neither a rival to nor a substitute for the best that medical care can give, but a support and complement to it. At times it may even be the decisive factor in recovery.

Our Lord specifically commissioned His disciples to heal the sick, and sent them forth empowered to do so. The Book of Acts gives us many instances of the apostles' work of healing. From the earliest times the care of the sick was an important element in the Church's ministry.

The method used always involved both the spoken word and (with the exception of mental cases) the touch of the hand. The spoken word might be exhortation or command; more often it was prayer. The healing touch might be either the laying on of hands, or an anointing with oil, or both. Where needed, the bestowal of Absolution was given. By the end of the first century the apostolic ministry of healing had passed to the official ministry of the Church, as is testified by the Epistle of James (5:14-15). In a preceding chapter we have noted second century testimony, from St. Justin Martyr,[3] that it was also customary for the deacons to take Holy Communion to the sick and others who were unable to be present with the Church at its regular celebrations of the Eucharist.

In the early Church the ministry to the sick, whether by laying on of hands or by unction (i.e., anointing), was viewed as a sacrament of healing. Its primary purpose was to restore the sick to wholeness of life and renewed participation in the corporate life of the Church. Unfortunately, in medieval times in the West, the Church's healing offices were transformed both in spirit and in purpose. The administration of Unction and Holy Communion to those who were sick was for the most part restricted to the dying, and considered to be "last rites" preparing them for the future life. Moreover, sickness in general was considered a mark of God's punishment for sin or a trial by God of a man's patience. Such views, of course, have no warrant in the teaching of the New Testament. God is never the author or giver of evil. Sickness may be indeed a result of sin; but it is never a visitation of God.

The medieval outlook was carried over into the Prayer

[3] See p. 74.

Book Office for the Visitation of the Sick, and even the Communion of the Sick. "Its whole tone," says a recent study of the office, "was not of encouragement, but of resignation. It did not exclude hope of recovery; but it was constructed throughout with the purpose of making systematic preparation for imminent death." [4] Recent revision of the office has done much to remove these weaknesses. Even so, the Visitation Office is seldom used in the exact form in which it appears in the Prayer Book, although its materials are freely adapted by the clergy in their ministrations. The provision of Unction, restored to the Prayer Book in 1928, is being more and more used, both in private and in public services, as our people are being trained to look upon it as a healing power, rather than as a last rite. Similarly, the administration of the Holy Communion to sick and shut-in persons has become once again one of the most constant assistances of the Church to such persons. It cannot be emphasized too strongly that the Communion of the Sick is, like Unction, a means of grace for this life no less than for the life to come.

The Visitation rite consists of a series of Psalms and Collects, to which other devotions may be added, as the minister deems best. Where needful, the minister speaks in his own words to the sick person "on the meaning and use of the time of sickness, and the opportunity it affords for spiritual profit" (Prayer Book, p. 313). Provision is also made for the sick to make a confession of sin and to receive Absolution, after which the office closes with a commendatory prayer and a blessing. In the case of those

[4] *Prayer Book Studies III: The Order for the Ministration to the Sick,* New York: The Church Pension Fund, 1951, p. 10.

who are dying, special prayers, a litany, absolution and final commendation are appointed (Prayer Book, pp. 317-19).

Unction may be used either in connection with the foregoing Office, or as a separate rite. The Prayer Book allows both forms employed in New Testament times: an anointing with oil, or laying on of hands. It should be especially noted that the words of this rite look forward to restoration "to soundness of health" and the return of the sick person to the fellowship of the Church, to offer "praise and thanksgiving."

The liturgy of healing is, of necessity, often administered privately. But it is none the less a corporate liturgy. Not only is the priest present as the representative of the whole Church, but lay persons are not excluded from participation in the Psalms and prayers. The rite of Unction may actually take place publicly in the church, for persons whose illness is not so severe as to prevent their attendance there. The rubrics of the Communion of the Sick imply that persons other than the priest and sick patient should be present and receive the sacrament with them. It is surely one of the greatest sources of strength to the sick to have such visible witness to the love and concern of the members of the Body one for another.

Is any sick among you? let him call for the elders of the church; and let them pray over him, anointing him with oil in the name of the Lord: And the prayer of faith shall save the sick, and the Lord shall raise him up; and if he have committed sins, they shall be forgiven him. Confess your faults one to another, and pray one for another, that ye may be healed. The effectual fervent prayer of a righteous man availeth much. (James 5:14-16.)

Such indeed is the action of the liturgy: to heal and to pardon, to restore and to unite.

BURIAL OF THE DEAD

We have noted in a preceding chapter[5] how the Easter faith of the Church has given to the memory of its departed members a hope and joy that is unique. We "sorrow not, even as others which have no hope. For if we believe that Jesus died and rose again, even so them also which sleep in Jesus will God bring with him" (I Thess. 4:13-14). The burial of a Christian is one of the sublime experiences of the Christian fellowship; for it marks the fulfillment of his Baptism in Christ's death that he might live with Him in the glory of His resurrection.

The most ancient funeral rite of the Church is the Requiem celebration of the Eucharist (Prayer Book, pp. 268-69).[6] It is also the most ancient memorial service. By the middle of the fourth century other rites had been developed in addition to the Requiem. Those that survive in the Prayer Book are: the funeral procession (either into the church or toward the grave); a special form of the Daily Offices, with appropriate Psalms, lesson, and prayers; and a committal to the grave. The Prayer Book also provides an additional set of these rites, with suitable Psalms, lesson, and prayers, for the Burial of a Child. The special Order for the Burial of the Dead, like the Requiem, may also be used independently as a memorial service.

The materials of these Offices of the Dead are taken

---

[5] See Chapter V.

[6] The word *Requiem* is derived from the opening word of the Introit in the Latin Mass for the Dead: "Rest eternal grant them, O Lord; and may light perpetual shine upon them."

almost entirely from the Scriptures. There is sounded through these forms the valiant faith of Job, the Psalmist's trust in God as a safe refuge, the Apostle's conviction that death has lost its sting and the grave its victory, the seer of Patmos' vision of the blessed rest of those who die in the Lord, and, above all, the assurance of our Lord Himself that whosoever liveth and believeth on Him shall never die. There is no service in all the Prayer Book that is so permeated from beginning to end with the spirit of joy and triumph and everlasting glory.

The Burial Offices assure us that death does not interrupt or break the fellowship of the Church. Our companionship in prayer and service continues with those who have entered into the "larger life." We pray for them, as we know they continue to pray for us, both the enjoyment of peace and contentment in God's presence and growth in His love and service.[7] We pray that we may have grace to follow their good examples, and that the work God has begun in us, as He has in them, may be perfected and found acceptable at the great Day when the secrets of all hearts shall be judged.

The lessons and prayers of the burial liturgy are very restrained in what they suggest about an "intermediate state" of the departed between the time of their death and the final Resurrection at the end of time. We are not encouraged to speculate about this mystery, nor about the way "the earth and the sea shall give up their dead" at Christ's coming, "and the corruptible bodies of those who sleep in him shall be changed, and made like unto his own glorious body." We are only assured that they

---

[7] See *The Faith of the Church*, pp. 179-82, for a discussion of prayer for the departed.

are in God's hands and that no power can take them from His keeping. "Blessed is the man," said St. Augustine, "who loves thee, O God, and his friend in Thee . . . For he alone loses no one who is dear to him, if all are dear in Him who never can be lost." [8]

---

[8] Augustine, *Confessions*, iv. 9.

CHAPTER TEN

The Ministry of the Church

AGAIN AND AGAIN, within the course of these chapters, we have been reminded that the liturgical worship of the Church is the responsibility of all its members, both the clergy and the laity. It is a corporate action of the entire Church, not a performance by the ordained ministry for the benefit of the people in the pews. Yet there is a special responsibility borne by the clergy because it is their duty to lead and preside over the Church's liturgical offices. This privilege they bear in a twofold capacity.

On the one hand they are chosen agents of the people in presenting before God the prayers and oblations of the Church. Their voice in the liturgy is a representative one. They speak in the name of the people. Their call to this ministry must be ratified by the people before they can be ordained to their sacred function, and their service in the worship of God is possible only in so far as the people are confident that they are duly empowered to act for them.

The authority of the clergy, however, does not derive from the people or congregations whom they serve. They are ministers of Christ in His Church. They have His call and His commission, which are prior to all other considerations. Their commission is given by others, who in their turn have received it in unbroken succession from the apostles. And the apostles received their call and commission from the Lord Himself.

In this chapter we shall consider first the means whereby the apostolic ministry is continued in the Church, and second the nature of the ministry of all those who are united with that apostolic ministry in the fellowship of the Church.

THE APOSTOLIC MINISTRY

Our Lord selected from among His followers twelve men, and commissioned them to carry on His work of preaching, teaching and healing. At the Last Supper He gave them a sacramental memorial of His redeeming sacrifice, which He commanded them to continue. In His Resurrection appearance to them, He gave them full power to carry His own ministry into all the world and to bear authority in His Name. "As my Father hath sent me, even so send I you . . . Receive ye the Holy Ghost" (John 20:21-22). Thus they were made *apostles,* i.e., men who are sent, men sent forth with the authority of Him who commissioned them. In addition, He chose other apostles, such as St. Paul, to bear His ministry among the Gentiles, in the power of the Holy Spirit.

The apostles literally planted the visible, historic Church. From the beginning they were accepted by all who believed their gospel message as authoritative leaders in doctrine, discipline and worship. They were the teachers, pastors and priests of the whole Church, and their decisions, made in counsel with the people, were accorded the highest spiritual authority.

As the Church grew in numbers and extent, the apostles

needed assistants in their ministry, and, in particular, representatives qualified to act for them in the churches they had founded. The Book of Acts and the New Testament Epistles give us some indications of this extension of the apostles' ministry. We cannot, however, recover all the details of it. But at the close of the apostolic age there had crystallized a threefold order of ministry, known as bishops, presbyters (later called priests) and deacons.[1]

The bishops were men ordained with the full authority of the apostles, and were accounted as their successors. Only bishops could ordain or consecrate other bishops. To them were entrusted the continuation of the apostolic ministry and the right to ordain the other ministries of the Church. The bishops bore responsibility for the preservation in the Church of the apostles' teaching; they had supervision of the pastoral work of the Church, and they presided, whenever present, over the liturgical worship of the congregations.

The presbyters served both as a council of advice to the bishop, and as his delegates in the general oversight of the church congregations. In the bishop's absence they presided over the liturgy. But they had no right to ordain, though in the ordination of men to their own ministry they joined with the bishop in the laying on of hands. The deacons were assistants of the bishop in the charitable work of pastoral care, and helped in the administration of the sacraments. But they could not preside over the Eucharist or confer absolution or blessing upon the people.

The ordination of all three orders of the ministry has

---

[1] See *The Holy Scriptures*, pp. 166-67; *Chapters in Church History*, pp. 38-42; and *The Faith of the Church*, pp. 137-40, 160.

always been, since apostolic times, by the laying on of hands with prayer. In the early Church it was customary for three bishops, at least, to join in the consecration of a new bishop. A bishop, assisted by his presbyters, ordained a new presbyter; and deacons were ordained by a bishop alone. The ordinations took place on Sundays or Holy Days, except in cases of necessity, and were performed within the course of the eucharistic liturgy. The consent of the people was always received before a man was admitted to any of the three Holy Orders. These customs and regulations of the ancient Church are still in force in our Episcopal Church today.

As the Church grew in numbers, and the area of the bishop's spiritual oversight increased in extent, the responsibility for teaching, pastoral care and corporate worship in the several congregations fell most heavily upon the presbyters, or, as we commonly call them, the parish priests. But the pre-eminence of the bishop's ministry has continued unchanged. Not only does he still preside over all ordinations, he also completes the initiation of a Christian by the laying on of hands in Confirmation. And whenever he is present at the eucharistic assembly, in any of the congregations under his diocesan care, he performs the priestly acts of pronouncing the Absolution and the Blessing. The bishop is still the final arbiter, in accordance with the Church's law, in questions of discipline both of the clergy and of the laity; and he makes final judgment with regard to admission to communion.

THE ORDINAL

During the Middle Ages the simplicity of the ancient ordination rites was lost sight of, and many picturesque, though edifying, ceremonies were added to the fundamental act of laying on of hands with prayer. The candidates for ordination were presented with the symbols of their office—the deacons with a book of the Gospels, the priests with a paten and chalice, and the bishops with a ring and pastoral staff. The hands of priests and bishops were anointed, as the hymn *Veni, Creator Spiritus* ("Come, Holy Ghost, our souls inspire") was solemnly chanted. The ordination prayer became detached from the laying on of hands, and in its place was substituted an imperative form, such as "Receive the Holy Ghost," etc. The result of this complication was confusion concerning the essential elements of the rites. And further perplexity was created by the variations of rite from diocese to diocese— an inevitable difficulty, of course, when books were all copied by hand, and local authorities were allowed to adapt traditional uses to suit their tastes or convictions.

The year following the issue of the first Prayer Book of 1549, Archbishop Cranmer issued an English *Ordinal*, containing simplified, vernacular liturgies for the ordination of bishops, priests, and deacons. This *Ordinal* has received some minor revisions in the course of time. But its rites remain substantially the same as those of the 1550 book throughout the provinces of the Anglican Communion.[2] Though many of the medieval ceremonies are retained or slightly modified in the English *Ordinal*, the striking characteristic is the clearness with which the New Testament emphasis upon the laying on of hands with prayer stands out as the essential act. But above everything

---

[2] The *Ordinal* of the American Prayer Book also contains two other rites, generally conducted by the bishop; The Form of Consecration of a Church or Chapel, and An Office of Institution of Ministers into Parishes or Churches. (Prayer Book, pp. 563-74.)

else, the English *Ordinal* is marked, both in the examinations of the candidates for all three orders and in the exhortations made to them, by an insistence upon the Scriptures as the norm by which the ministry is to teach the Christian Faith and to set an example of Christian living. Each of the three rites of ordination is embodied within the Eucharistic celebration. And in each rite a sermon is required, declaring the duties of the several orders of ministry, their necessity in the Church, and the esteem which the people should have for them.

The structure of the three ordination rites is similar, though each one has its own peculiar characteristics of detail. In the ordination of deacons and priests, the sermon comes first, followed by the presentation of the candidates, the charge of the bishop to the congregation as to the candidates' fitness, and the Litany.[3] The Communion rite is then begun. The deacon's examination and ordination is inserted after the Epistle; the priest's, after the Gospel. Both deacons and priests may be ordained at the same service. At the Consecration of bishops, the Ante-Communion precedes the sermon, and the ordination is placed between the sermon and the Offertory.

The deacon's ordination is very simple. After the Epistle has been read, the bishop gives the candidate a public examination respecting his call, his faith, and his readiness to fulfill the duties of his office. An ordination prayer should normally follow at this point, but one of the accidents of history is that this prayer is deferred to a later time. It is read just before the final Blessing of the Com-

---

[3] Either the General Litany (Prayer Book, pp. 54-59), or, more commonly, the special Litany for Ordinations (Prayer Book, pp. 560-62). This latter was an addition of the 1928 Prayer Book.

munion (pp. 534-35). The laying on of hands follows immediately upon the examination. The deacon is then presented a copy of the New Testament, and begins to exercise his duties at once by reading the Gospel lesson of the Eucharist.

The ordering of a priest is distinguished by a magnificent exhortation read by the bishop immediately following the Gospel lesson, after which the bishop proceeds to examine the candidate. Silent prayer is then offered by the whole congregation "for a space," whereupon the bishop intones, antiphonally with the people, the *Veni, Creator Spiritus.* The ordination prayer is read by the bishop, and then with the other priests present he bestows the laying on of hands. The new priest is presented with a copy of the Bible.

The consecration of a bishop is similar to the ordering of a priest. But there are these differences. Immediately after the bishop-elect is presented to the Presiding Bishop, public testimonials are read with respect to the candidate's proper qualifications and election to his office. Then in the presence of the clergy and laity the bishop-elect takes a solemn oath of his "conformity and obedience to the Doctrine, Discipline, and Worship of the Protestant Episcopal Church in the United States of America." [4] There is no exhortation preceding the examination, as in the ordering of priests; but after his consecration he receives, as did the priest, a copy of the Bible.

It is clear from these brief summaries of the ordination liturgy that the Episcopal Church carefully maintains the

---

[4] Similar testimonials and oaths are required by the Canons of the Church for those ordained deacons and priests; but they are received by the bishop before the ordination rite takes place.

orders of ministry "that from the Apostles' time" have existed in Christ's Church. And it holds these orders "in such reverend estimation, that no man might presume to execute any of them, except he were first called, tried, examined, and known to have such qualities as are requisite for the same; and also by public Prayer, with Imposition of Hands, were approved and admitted thereunto by lawful Authority." [5] What the Church considers to be the ideal character and work of the Ministry may be readily seen in the examinations included in each of the ordination rites, and above all, in the exhortation the bishop reads at the ordering of priests (pp. 539-41). These paragraphs are unexcelled, both for their matchless elevation and dignity of style, and for their heart-searching account of the responsibility of the ministry "to be Messengers, Watchmen, and Stewards of the Lord."

THE PRIESTHOOD OF THE LAITY

The Church of our Lord Jesus Christ is described in the New Testament sometimes as a body, sometimes as a building. The thought behind these metaphors is that of a unified structure, made up of many parts. Yet each part must fit into its own proper place in relation to all the other parts; nor can any single unit have value apart from its function in relation to the whole. Moreover, all the parts are necessary to the well-being of the whole, since each part both supports and depends upon all the others. Christ is Himself the source of unity, upon whom all the parts depend, whether He be likened to the head of the body, or to the foundation or corner stone of the building.

---

[5] From the Preface of the *Ordinal,* p. 529.

Without Him the whole structure disintegrates and falls apart.

The figure is further developed by the New Testament writers—one might say, given animation—by the conception of the indwelling Spirit of the Lord in the body, or in the building, as the case may be. The Spirit not only makes the structure alive to its God-given purpose; He imparts to each of its several members or parts its own peculiar service to the whole. Thus, in a classic passage of St. Paul, we read of the gifts of the Spirit to the members of the body:

> Now there are diversities of gifts, but the same Spirit.
> And there are differences of administrations, but the same
>   Lord.
> And there are diversities of operations, but it is the same
>   God which worketh all in all.
> But the manifestation of the Spirit is given to every man
>   to profit withal.
> For to one is given by the Spirit the word of wisdom;
>   to another the word of knowledge by the same Spirit;
>   to another faith by the same Spirit;
>   to another the gifts of healing by the same Spirit;
>   to another the working of miracles;
>   to another prophecy;
>   to another discerning of spirits;
>   to another divers kinds of tongues;
>   to another the interpretation of tongues:
> but all these worketh that one and the selfsame Spirit,
>   dividing to every man severally as he will.
> For as the body is one, and hath many members, and all
>   the members of that one body, being many, are one
>   body: so also is Christ. (I Cor. 12:4-12.)

Similarly, in the first Epistle of Peter, the figure of the building as a "spiritual house" is presented:

Ye also, as lively stones, are built up a spiritual house, an holy priesthood, to offer up spiritual sacrifices, acceptable to God by Jesus Christ. Wherefore also it is contained in the scripture, Behold, I lay in Sion a chief corner stone, elect, precious: and he that believeth on him shall not be confounded. (I Peter 2:5-6.)

Every member of the Church, because he is a member of Christ and receives from Christ His Holy Spirit, is in truth a minister—a minister of his own spiritual gifts to all the other members. This ministry is received by each and every one of us in our initiation into Christ, when we are incorporated into His Body, the Church, and endowed with the Spirit's sevenfold gifts of grace. Our ministry is not exercised solely within the fellowship of the Body, but in all our several vocations and occupations in the world. It is a ministry of witness to Christ and of service to His cause, bringing men and women to faith in Him, and responding to their needs in sacrificial giving of our talents and labor. This is the ministry for which we pray in the Good Friday Collect:

Almighty and everlasting God, by whose Spirit the whole body of the Church is governed and sanctified; Receive our supplications and prayers, which we offer before thee for all estates of men in thy holy Church, that every member of the same, in his vocation and ministry, may truly and godly serve thee; through our Lord and Saviour Jesus Christ. *Amen*. (Prayer Book, pp. 156-57.)

The highest privilege of our common ministry is to offer the service of our lives to one another and to God in the liturgy, and in particular, in the Eucharistic sacrifice. For in this action our Lord, who is our great High

Priest, makes us sharers in His redeeming work for the reconciliation of God and men. The priestly office is in its essence a "ministry of reconciliation." It is a ministry that seeks to bring all the good things of God's created world, all the relationships of our daily lives, and all the desires and hopes of human hearts, into harmony and conformity with that will which is perfect righteousness, love and peace. This is none other than the ministry of our Lord, working mightily by His Spirit in us and through us, that we may offer with Him unto God and our Father an acceptable sacrifice. "Unto him that loved us, and washed us from our sins in his own blood, and hath made us kings and priests unto God and his Father; to him be glory and dominion for ever and ever. *Amen.*" (Rev. 1:5-6.)

About the Authors

The Rev. Massey H. Shepherd, Jr., S.T.D., is Professor of Church History at Episcopal Theological School and associate rector of St. John's Church, Roxbury, Mass. A graduate of Berkeley Divinity School and the University of South Carolina, he received his Ph.D. from the University of Chicago, where he was Instructor in Divinity from 1937 to 1940. Dr. Shepherd was formerly minister-in-charge of the Church of Our Saviour, Allerton, Mass. and is a past president of the American Society of Church History. Among his books are: *The Oxford American Prayer Book Commentary, The Living Liturgy* and *At All Times and In All Places.*

OTHER MEMBERS OF THE AUTHORS' COMMITTEE AT THE TIME THIS BOOK WAS WRITTEN

The Rev. Thomas J. Bigham, Jr., S.T.M., is Instructor in Ethics at General Theological Seminary. He is co-author of *Christ With Us* and author of *To The Soul's Health.*

The Rev. Stanley Brown-Serman, D.D., S.T.D., formerly Professor of New Testament Language and Literature at the Theological Seminary, Alexandria, Va., attended Keble College, Oxford, and Columbia University. He is the co-author of *What Did Jesus Think?* Dr. Brown-Serman recently went to Brazil to assist the faculty of the theological seminary there in setting up a long range program.

The Rev. Powel Mills Dawley, Ph.D., is Professor of Ecclesiastical History at the General Theological Seminary. A graduate of Brown University and the Episcopal Theological School, Cambridge, Mass., he received his Ph.D. from Cambridge University, England. He is the author of *Chapters in Church History* and is currently at work, with the Rev. James T. Addison, on *The Episcopal Church at Work,* sixth volume in the CHURCH'S TEACHING series.

The Rev. Robert Claude Dentan, Ph.D., is Professor of the Literature and Interpretation of the Old Testament at the Berkeley Divinity School, New Haven, Conn. A graduate of Colorado College and Berkeley Divinity School, he received his Ph.D. from Yale University. He was formerly priest-in-charge of St. John's Church, Donora, Pa., and rector of St. John's Church, New Haven, Conn. He is the author of *The Holy Scriptures.*

The Rev. Frederick W. Dillistone, D.D., formerly Professor of Theology at Episcopal Theological School, is Canon of Liverpool Cathedral. A graduate of Oxford, he has taught at Wycliffe College and London College of Divinity. His books include *The Significance of the Cross, The Holy Spirit in Life Today, Revelation and Evangelism.* He was a joint editor of the *Westminster Study Bible.*

The Rev. Joseph F. Fletcher, 3rd, S.T.D., is Professor of Pastoral Theology and Christian Ethics at Episcopal Theological School, Cambridge. Chairman of the Association of Christian Social Ethics Professors, he is the author of *The Church and Industry* and *Christianity and Property.*

The Rev. Reuel L. Howe, S.T.D., is Professor of Pastoral Theology at the Theological Seminary, Alexandria, Va.

The author of *The Need for a Ministry to the Pre-School Child,* he is now at work on *Man's Need and God's Answer.*

The Rev. John Heuss, D.D., formerly Director, the Department of Christian Education of the National Council, and co-chairman of this series of books, is rector of Trinity Church, New York.

The Rev. David R. Hunter, Ed.D., formerly head of the Department of Christian Education, Diocese of Massachusetts, is Director of the Department of Christian Education of the National Council and co-chairman of this series of books.

Leon McCauley, publishing consultant to the Authors' Committee, is manager of The Seabury Press, Inc.

The Rev. Albert Theodore Mollegen, D.D., is Professor of Christian Ethics at the Theological Seminary, Alexandria, Va., where he has been on the teaching staff since 1936. He was ordained in 1932 and received his D.D. from the University of the South. He has contributed to *Anglican Evangelicalism.*

The Rev. C. Kilmer Myers is Vicar of St. Augustine's Chapel, Trinity Parish, New York. A graduate of Rutgers University and Berkeley Divinity School, he has been an Instructor in Liturgics at Berkeley and General Theological Seminary. He is the author of *Liturgy and Life, The Church and the Seminary,* and *Unity through Liturgy.*

The Very Rev. James A. Pike, J.S.D., Dean of the Cathedral of St. John the Divine, New York. After taking his doctorate in law from Yale, he practiced for six years before his ordination. Most recently he was Chaplain and Chairman of the Department of Religion at Columbia University. He is co-author of *The Faith of the Church.*

The Rev. W. Norman Pittenger, S.T.D., is Professor of Apologetics at the General Theological Seminary. He has been on the teaching staff of the seminary since his graduation from that institution in 1936, and has served as Lecturer in Religion at Columbia University. He is the author of a number of theological books, and is the co-author of *The Faith of the Church.*

The Rev. Frederick Q. Shafer is Lecturer in Religion at the University of the South in Sewanee, Tenn. He is a graduate of Bard College and the General Theological Seminary.

The Rev. Charles William Frederick Smith, D.D., is Professor of New Testament at Episcopal Theological School. He was formerly rector of St. Andrew's Church, Wellesley, Mass., and is chairman of the Department of Christian Education of the Diocese of Massachusetts. Ordained in 1933, he is a graduate of the Theological Seminary, Alexandria, Va., and the University of Virginia. He is the author of *The Jesus of the Parables.*

The Rev. William A. Spurrier, 3rd, B.D., is Assistant Professor of Religion and associate pastor at Wesleyan College, Middletown, Conn. He is the author of *Power for Action,* and is currently at work on *Christian Living,* the fifth volume in the CHURCH's TEACHING series.

The Rev. Vesper O. Ward, D.D., S.T.D., is Editor in Chief for Curriculum Development in the Department of Christian Education of the National Council.

The Rev. Theodore O. Wedel, Ph.D., is Warden of the College of Preachers in Washington, D.C. He is a graduate of Oberlin College and took his Ph.D. at Yale in 1918. He was Professor of English at Carleton College from 1922 to 1934, and Secretary for College Work of the National Council, 1934 to 1939. He is the author of *The Coming Great Church.*

Bibliography

PART ONE:
THE PRINCIPLES OF CHRISTIAN
WORSHIP

GENERAL WORKS:

Worship by Evelyn Underhill (New York: Harpers, 1937).
A comprehensive analysis of the nature of worship, with an
interpretation of its expression in Judaism and the various
traditions of Christendom, Eastern and Western, Catholic,
Anglican and Reformed. A difficult book for the average
reader, but a rewarding one for those who study it closely.

Our Heritage in Public Worship by D. H. Hislop (Edinburgh:
T. and T. Clark, 1935). Covers much the same ground as
Miss Underhill's work, but is simpler in style. Gives more
attention to psychological factors in worship.

The Way of Worship, A Study in Ecumenical Recovery by
Scott Francis Brenner (New York: Macmillan, 1944). A
contribution to the cause of Christian unity by way of the
central elements of the historic worship of the Church. For
the general reader.

Prayer, A Study in the History and Psychology of Religion by
Friedrich Heiler (New York: Oxford University Press, 1932).
An encyclopedic work, studying the varieties of prayer in
pagan and Christian worship, both private and public.
Viewpoint that "prayer is the central phenomenon of re-
ligion."

*Liturgy and Society, The Function of the Church in the Mod-
ern World* by A. G. Hebert (London: Faber and Faber,

Ltd., 1935). An essay on the relation of the Church's liturgy to the modern world. A fundamental work.

CHAPTER ONE:
THE MOTIVES FOR CORPORATE WORSHIP

Reality in Worship, A Study of Public Worship and Private Religion by Willard L. Sperry (New York: Macmillan, 1926). Written primarily for non-liturgical churches in America, this book is an acute analysis of motives, ideals, and needs of corporate worship in the modern age.

Living Worship by David G. Peck (London: Eyre and Spottiswoode, 1944). An interpretation of the relevance of corporate worship to the modern world.

Worship, Its Social Significance, edited by P. T. R. Kirk (London: Centenary Press, 1939). The relevance of worship to modern social problems.

Church Worship and the Non-Churchgoer, A Handbook for Clergy and Teachers (London: S.P.C.K., 1944). Practical suggestions on how to teach liturgical worship in our times.

CHAPTER TWO:
THE ELEMENTS OF CORPORATE WORSHIP

Worship by J. O. Dobson (London: SCM Press, 1941). A solid presentation of the subject for popular reading.

Ideas in Corporate Worship by Robert Stephenson Simpson (Edinburgh: T. and T. Clark, 1927).

The Sacraments and the Church, A Study in the Corporate Nature of Christianity by Henry de Candole (London: Mowbray, 1935). A simple introduction for the general reader.

The Christian Sacraments by Oliver Chase Quick (New York: Harpers, 1927). A more advanced theological work.

See also the general bibliography to Part One and the titles listed under the following chapter.

CHAPTER THREE:
LITURGICAL WORSHIP

Ways of Worship edited by Pehr Edwall, Eric Hayman, and William D. Maxwell. The Report of a Theological Commission of Faith and Order (New York: Harpers, 1951). A symposium of eminent leaders of all denominations which examines the elements of liturgy, the inner meanings of Word and Sacrament, and the relation of liturgy and devotion, within the several branches of Christendom.

Liturgical Prayer, Its History and Spirit by Fernand Cabrol (Westminster, Md.: Newman Press, 1950). A detailed study of the origins of liturgical forms and usages, with special reference to the early Roman Catholic liturgy.

The Worship of the English Puritans by Horton Davies (Westminster: Dacre Press, 1948). A history of the origins of Puritan dissent from the liturgy of the Book of Common Prayer.

The Art of Public Worship by Percy Dearmer (London: Mowbray, 1919). A study of the Prayer Book liturgy, both in theory and practice, from the viewpoint that "the common worship of God is an art."

The Spirit of the Liturgy by Romano Guardini (London: Sheed and Ward, 1930). A classic interpretation of the purpose and meaning of liturgical worship by a Roman Catholic scholar.

Liturgical Worship by Joseph A. Jungmann (New York: Frederick Pustet Co., Inc., 1941). Another brief explanation of the meaning of liturgy by an eminent Roman Catholic Jesuit.

The Principles of Religious Ceremonial by Walter Howard Frere (New edition; London: Mowbray, 1928). The standard work on ceremonial, analyzing its various purposes, and illustrating these by reference to the historic rites of the East and West.

ARCHITECTURE:

A History of Religious Architecture by Ernest H. Short (New York: Macmillan, 1936). A standard reference history of the various styles and monuments of religious architecture.

The Architectural Setting of Anglican Worship by G. W. O. Addleshaw and Frederick Etchells (London: Faber and Faber, Ltd., 1948). The subtitle reads: "An Inquiry into the Arrangements for Public Worship in the Church of England from the Reformation to the Present Day."

The Church Architecture of Protestantism by Andrew L. Drummond (Edinburgh: T. and T. Clark, 1934). An historical and constructive survey of church architecture of all denominations, both in Europe and America.

Church Building, A Study of the Principles of Architecture in Their Relation to the Church by Ralph Adams Cram (3rd edition; Boston: Marshall Jones Co., 1924). A critique of church building in America in the last generation, by one of our greatest architects.

The Church of Tomorrow by William Ward Watkin (New York: Harpers, 1936). Contains excellent suggestions as to site, size, plan, materials and fixtures of new church buildings.

MUSIC:

Sacred Music by Alec Robertson (New York: Chanticleer Press, 1950). An illustrated outline of the history of church music from apostolic times to the present.

The Singing Church, An Outline History of the Music Sung by Choir and People by C. Henry Phillips (London: Faber and Faber, Ltd., 1945). A brief survey of the various types and styles of music used in the liturgy of the Church through the ages.

Church Music in History and Practice, Studies in the Praise of God by Winfred Douglas (The Hale Lectures; New

York: Scribners, 1937). The standard textbook on the history and use of music in the American Episcopal Church, with extensive lists of recordings, and bibliography.

Quires and Places Where They Sing by S. Nicholson (London: G. Bell and Sons, 1932). A practical handbook for leaders of church music in cathedrals and parishes.

Music and Worship by Walford Davies and Harvey Grace (New York: H. W. Gray Co., 1935). A reliable guide to selection and performance of music in the Church's worship.

Church Music, Illusion and Reality by Archibald T. Davison (Cambridge: Harvard University Press, 1952). An historical and aesthetic critique of present-day standards of music used in church services.

Report of the Joint Commission on Church Music, 1930 (New York: H. W. Gray Co.).

Music in Church. A Report of a Committee appointed in 1948 by the Archbishops of Canterbury and York (Westminster: The Church Information Board, 1951).

Official statements and analyses of the use of music in the Prayer Book services, in the United States and in England.

CHAPTER FOUR:
THE HERITAGE OF THE LITURGY

The general bibliographies to both Part One and Part Two should be consulted. Many of the books there listed give surveys of the history of the Church's rites and ceremonies.

GENERAL SURVEYS:

Christian Worship by F. C. Burkitt (Cambridge: Cambridge University Press, 1930). A simple, brief and reliable account.

A History of Christian Worship by Oscar Hardman (London: Hodder and Stoughton, 1937). A standard textbook for the general reader.

The Church at Prayer and the World Outside by Percy Dearmer (Boston: The Pilgrim Press, 1923). An interpretation for modern men of the various types of corporate worship from New Testament times to the present day.

The Spirit of Worship, Its Forms and Manifestations in the Christian Churches by Friedrich Heiler, translated by W. Montgomery (New York: George H. Doran Co., 1926). A study of "unity in diversity" in the historic liturgies of the chief branches of the Church.

An Outline of Christian Worship, Its Development and Forms by William D. Maxwell (New York: Oxford University Press, 1936). Traces the history of the form of the liturgy, especially the Holy Communion, from its origin to the present day. Contains a fine bibliography.

Christian Worship, Studies in Its History and Meaning by Members of Mansfield College, edited by Nathaniel Micklem (Oxford: Clarendon Press, 1936). A series of scholarly essays on the philosophy, history, and practice of Christian worship from Biblical times to the present. The treatment of the Protestant Reformers is especially noteworthy, though there is no discussion of Anglican traditions.

The Shape of the Liturgy by Dom Gregory Dix (Westminster: Dacre Press, 1945). A monumental work, containing chapters both of a popular and of a technical character, covering the history of the liturgy through the Reformation period. Some of its interpretations should be used with caution, especially the treatment of Cranmer's work (see *Zwingli and Cranmer on the Eucharist* by Cyril C. Richardson [Evanston: Seabury-Western Theological Seminary, 1949]).

English Prayer Books, An Introduction to the Literature of Christian Public Worship (3rd edition; New York: Cambridge University Press, 1949). A succinct and readable survey of the various liturgical books and publications used in England since the time of the conversion of the English people.

The Jewish Background of the Christian Liturgy by W. O. E. Oesterley (Oxford: Clarendon Press, 1925). Valuable for its presentation of Jewish sources; but the author's theory about the occasion of the Last Supper is not generally accepted.

The Jewish Antecedents of the Christian Sacraments by Frank Gavin (London: S.P.C.K., 1928). An important discussion of the sources of Christian liturgy.

Christian Worship in the Primitive Church by Alexander B. Macdonald (Edinburgh: T. and T. Clark, 1934). A readable and comprehensive presentation of worship in the apostolic age.

The Early History of the Liturgy by J. H. Srawley (2nd edition; New York: Cambridge University Press, 1947). A convenient summary of recent scholarship. Treats chiefly of the Holy Communion.

Christian Worship, Its Origin and Evolution by L. Duchesne, translated by M. L. McClure (London: S.P.C.K., 1903). A fundamental introduction to the history of the liturgy down to the ninth century. Some of its theories are no longer accepted.

The Mass of the Western Rites by Dom Fernand Cabrol, translated by C. M. Antony (St. Louis: B. Herder Book Co., 1934). A scholarly survey of the Roman and Gallican liturgies in their formation and development.

Some of the important sources dealing with the Church's worship in early times are conveniently available in English translation:

The Apostolic Tradition of Hippolytus. Translation with Introduction and Notes, by B. S. Easton (New York: Macmillan, 1934); and by Gregory Dix (London: S.P.C.K., 1937).

Bishop Sarapion's Prayer-Book. An Egyptian Sacramentary dated probably about A.D. 350-356. With Introduction, Notes, and Indices, by John Wordsworth (2nd edition; London: S.P.C.K., 1923).

St. Cyril of Jerusalem's Lectures on the Christian Sacraments edited by Frank Leslie Cross (London: S.P.C.K., 1951).

The Liturgy of the Eighth Book of 'The Apostolic Constitutions' commonly called The Clementine Liturgy by R. H. Cresswell (2nd edition; London: S.P.C.K., 1924).

St. Ambrose On the Sacraments and On the Mysteries, translated by T. Thompson, edited with Introduction and Notes by J. H. Srawley (2nd edition; London: S.P.C.K., 1950).

Western Liturgies by R. C. West (London: S.P.C.K., 1938). Translates examples of all the Western rites, Roman and Gallican.

The Orthodox Liturgy, Being the Divine Liturgy of S. John Chrysostom and S. Basil the Great. (London: S.P.C.K., 1939.) There are many other translations of these liturgies current.

Eastern Catholic Worship by Donald Attwater (New York: Devin-Adair Co., 1945). Translation of Greek, Armenian, Coptic, Ethiopic, Syrian liturgies, etc.

MEDIEVAL AND MODERN:

Church Services and Service-Books before the Reformation by Henry Barclay Swete (London: S.P.C.K., 1896). An introduction to the worship of the medieval Latin Church. Describes the various liturgical books in use before the Prayer Book.

The Sarum Missal in English, translated by Frederick E. Warren, 2 volumes (Alcuin Club Collections, XI; London: Mowbray, 1913). The basic source used by Cranmer in the compilation of the Prayer Book.

The Mass, A Study of the Roman Liturgy by Adrian Fortescue

(2nd edition; London: Longmans, Green and Co., 1937). A standard history of the Latin rite. Contains lengthy bibliography.

The Mass of the Roman Rite: Its Origins and Development by Joseph A. Jungmann, translated by Francis A. Brunner, 2 volumes (New York: Benziger Brothers, Inc., 1951). An encyclopedic and authoritative history and exposition of the Roman rite. With a lengthy bibliography and copious notes. For the specialist.

An Introduction to the Study of Eastern Liturgies by Sévérien Salaville, translated by John M. T. Barton (London: Sands and Co., 1938). A comprehensive guide for the general reader.

The Lutheran Liturgy, A Study of the Common Service of the Lutheran Church in America by Luther D. Reed (Philadelphia: Muhlenberg press, 1947). A standard and authoritative textbook on the Lutheran tradition of worship.

The Liturgy of the Church of Scotland since the Reformation by Stephen A. Hurlbut (Charleston: The St. Albans Press, 1952). Basic source material with competent notes on the principal liturgies of the Calvinistic tradition.

See Part Two for bibliography on the history of the Book of Common Prayer and the worship of the Anglican Communion.

PART TWO:
THE BOOK OF COMMON PRAYER

REFERENCE WORKS:

The Prayer Book Dictionary edited by George Harford and Morley Stevenson (New York: Longmans, Green and Co., 1912). Articles covering all phases of the history and contents of the Prayer Book.

The English Rite, Being a Synopsis of the Sources and Revi-sions of the Book of Common Prayer by F. E. Brightman, 2 volumes (London: Rivingtons, 1915). An authoritative source book, giving the origins of all forms and of all changes in the English Prayer Book in its 1549, 1552 and 1661 editions.

Liturgiae Americanae, or The Book of Common Prayer as used in the United States of America compared with the Proposed Book of 1786 and with the Prayer Book of the Church of England, and an Historical Account and Documents by William McGarvey (Philadelphia, 1895). A work on the American Prayer Book, similar to Brightman's on the English, through the 1892 revision.

The Book of Common Prayer among the Nations of the World by William Muss-Arnolt (London: S.P.C.K., 1914). "A History of Translations of the Prayer Book of the Church of England and of the Protestant Episcopal Church of America."

Liturgy and Worship, A Companion to the Prayer Books of the Anglican Communion edited by W. K. Lowther Clarke and Charles Harris (London: S.P.C.K., 1932). A storehouse of information about the history and contents of the Prayer Book. An indispensable guide book for all students of the Prayer Book.

COMMENTARIES:

The Annotated Book of Common Prayer, Being an Historical, Ritual, and Theological Commentary on the Devotional System of the Church of England by John Henry Blunt (Revised edition; New York: E. P. Dutton and Co., 1883). The most voluminous of all Prayer Book commentaries, still useful, but in some respects out of date.

The Teacher's Prayer Book . . . with Introductions, Analyses, Notes, and A Commentary upon the Psalter by Alfred

Barry (New York: Thomas Nelson and Sons, 1899). Designed for the layman, this old work is still useful for its devotional interpretations.

The Prayer-Book, Its History, Language, and Contents by Evan Daniel (20th edition; London: Wells, Gardner, Darton and Co., Ltd., 1901). Concise, dependable; especially good for explanation of words and phrases.

The Tutorial Prayer Book for the Teacher, the Student, and the General Reader edited by Charles Neil and M. Willoughby (London: The Harrison Trust, 1913). From a strongly evangelical viewpoint.

The Book of Common Prayer, with Commentary for Teachers and Students edited by F. E. Warren (2nd edition; London: S.P.C.K., 1922). Competent essays on all parts of the Prayer Book, with a glossary, and a concordance to the Psalter.

The Oxford American Prayer Book Commentary by Massey Hamilton Shepherd, Jr. (New York: Oxford University Press, 1950). The only commentary on the 1928 American Book. Page by page exposition of the entire Book, except for the Psalter, with an index of Scriptural passages contained in the Prayer Book.

HISTORY AND RATIONALE:

The following are *popular* introductions to the history and content of the Prayer Book:

The People's Book of Worship, A Study of the Book of Common Prayer by John Wallace Suter and Charles Morris Addison (New York: Macmillan, 1919).

The New American Prayer Book, Its History and Contents by E. Clowes Chorley (New York: Macmillan, 1930).

How the Prayer Book Came to Us, A History for Young People by Gertrude Hollis (London: The Faith Press, Ltd., 1928).

An Introduction to the Prayer Book by F. W. Vroom (New York: Macmillan, 1930).

The Romance of the Book of Common Prayer by Francis G. Burgess (Milwaukee: Morehouse Publishing Co., 1930).

The Story of the Prayer Book in the Old and New World and Throughout the Anglican Church by Percy Dearmer (New York: Oxford University Press, 1933). Profusely illustrated. A popular textbook in schools.

Prayer Book Interleaves by William Palmer Ladd (New York: Oxford University Press, 1942).

The Living Liturgy by Massey Hamilton Shepherd, Jr. (New York: Oxford University Press, 1946).

The Heart of the Prayer Book by William E. Cox (Richmond: The Dietz Press, Inc., 1944). Devotional in character.

The Book of Common Prayer, The Anglican Heritage of Public Worship by D. E. W. Harrison (London: Canterbury Press, 1946).

The Story of the Prayer Book in England and America by Verney Johnstone, with additional chapters by Ernest Evans and Leicester C. Lewis (New York: Morehouse-Gorham Co., 1949).

The American Book of Common Prayer, Its Origin and Development by John Wallace Suter and George Julius Cleaveland (New York: Oxford University Press, 1949).

The Booke of Common Prayer, Its Making and Revisions 1549-1661, by Edward C. Ratcliff (Alcuin Club Collections, XXXVII; London: S.P.C.K., 1949). With 80 plates, showing various editions of the Prayer Book.

The following are more detailed works of introduction:

The History of the Book of Common Prayer by Leighton Pullan (2nd edition; London: Longmans, Green and Co., 1900).

A New History of the Book of Common Prayer with a Rationale of Its Offices by Francis Procter and Walter Howard Frere (London: Macmillan, 1901).

The Book of Common Prayer by Samuel Hart (Sewanee: University Press, 1910). The standard work on the 1892 American Prayer Book.

Primitive Worship and the Prayer Book, Rationale, History, and Doctrine of the English, Irish, Scottish, and American Books by W. Gwynne (London: Longmans, Green and Co., 1917).

The American Prayer Book, Its Origins and Principles by Edward Lambe Parsons and Bayard Hale Jones (New York: Scribners, 1937). The standard work on the American Prayer Book, with an excellent bibliography.

SPECIAL TOPICS:

Cranmer's First Litany, 1544, and Merbecke's Book of Common Prayer Noted, 1550, by J. Eric Hunt (London: S.P.C.K., 1939). Contains facsimile reproductions of work of Merbecke, with an introduction.

A History of Conferences and Other Proceedings connected with the Revision of the Book of Common Prayer from the Year 1558 to the Year 1690 by Edward Cardwell (New York: Oxford University Press, 1849). An invaluable collection of source materials.

The Workmanship of the Prayer Book in its Literary and Liturgical Aspects by John Dowden (3rd edition; London: Methuen, 1904).

Further Studies in the Prayer Book by John Dowden (London: Methuen, 1908). Bishop Dowden's two books give important interpretations of the sources of Cranmer's work, and of his literary accomplishments in the Prayer Book.

The Prayer Book Reform Movement in the XVIIIth Century by A. Elliott Preston (Oxford: Basil Blackwood, 1940). A study of attempts at Prayer Book revision in the age of the Enlightenment.

The Book of Common Prayer and the Worship of the Non-

Anglican Churches by William D. Maxwell (New York: Oxford University Press, 1950). The influence of the Prayer Book on other religious bodies in England and Scotland.

Who Wrote the New Prayers in the Prayer Book? by James Arthur Muller (Philadelphia: Church Historical Society, 1946). Studies in the authorship of the prayers added to the American Book in 1928.

CEREMONIAL:

A Short Handbook of Public Worship in the Churches of the Anglican Communion by Percy Dearmer (Oxford University Press, 1931).

The Parson's Handbook by Percy Dearmer (Oxford University Press, 1928). More detailed than the preceding work.

The Ceremonial of the English Church by Vernon Staley (London: Mowbray, 1899). Traditional English ceremonial.

A Prayer Book Manual, prepared by the Boston Clergy Group of the Episcopal Evangelical Fellowship (Louisville: Cloister Press, 1943).

CHAPTER FIVE:
THE CHRISTIAN YEAR

The Church Year and Kalendar by John Dowden (Cambridge University Press, 1910). An introductory manual to the historical origins of the Church's feasts and fasts.

The Liturgical Year, An Explanation of the Origin, History and Significance of the Festival Days and Fasting Days of the English Church by Vernon Staley (London: Mowbray, 1907). An old book, but still a standard introduction for the general reader.

The Christian Year, Its Purpose and Its History by Walker Gwynne (New York: Longmans, Green and Co., 1915). Brief and reliable.

The Ministry of Grace by John Wordsworth (2nd edition;

London: Longmans, Green and Co., 1903). Contains some useful chapters on the origins of the Church Calendar.

The Year of Our Lord, The Mystery of Christ in the Liturgical Year by Emiliana Loehr (New York: P. J. Kenedy and Sons, 1937). A good example of Roman Catholic interpretation of the doctrinal teaching of the Christian Year.

Sunday by W. B. Trevelyan (London: Longmans, Green and Co., 1903). A study of the Christian meaning and use of the Lord's Day.

Studies in Early Roman Liturgy: I. The Kalendar by Walter Howard Frere (Alcuin Club Collections, XXVIII; Oxford University Press, 1930). A highly technical research into the origins of the Roman holy days, many of which are carried over into the Prayer Book Calendar.

Historical Survey of Holy Week, Its Services and Ceremonial by John Walton Tyrer (Alcuin Club Collections, XXIX; Oxford University Press, 1932). Detailed and technical account.

The Collects of the Day, An Exposition Critical and Devotional of the Collects appointed at the Communion by Edward Meyrick Goulburn, 2 volumes (New York: Pott, Young, and Co., 1880). This old work is still the best exposition of the doctrine and devotional meaning of the Prayer Book Collects.

The Eternal Word in the Modern World, Expository Preaching on the Gospels and Epistles for the Church Year by Burton Scott Easton and Howard Chandler Robbins (New York: Scribners, 1937). Expositions, both critical and homiletical, of the Epistles and Gospels, with much reliable information on the origin of the Christian Year.

Social Teachings of the Christian Year by Vida D. Scudder (New York: E. P. Dutton and Co., 1921). Devotional comments on the relevance of the seasons to Christian concern for social problems.

Prayer Book Studies: II. *The Liturgical Lectionary* (New York: The Church Pension Fund, 1950). Published by the Standing Liturgical Commission of the Episcopal Church, this study presents suggestions for revision of the schedule of Epistles and Gospels, with many illuminating notes on the Christian Year.

CHAPTER SIX:
MORNING AND EVENING PRAYER
AND THE LITANY

THE DAILY OFFICES:

Matins and Evensong by Clement F. Rogers (London: Faith Press, Ltd., 1924). A readable survey of the history of the Daily Offices, with some practical suggestions for their use today.

The Church's Prayers by Henry de Candole (London: Mowbray, 1939). The best exposition of the purpose and meaning of the Daily Offices as a corporate offering of praise to God.

Learning to Pray with the Church by Verney Johnstone (London: Longmans, Green and Co., 1949). A helpful guide to lay people to intelligent and meaningful participation in the Daily Offices.

The American Lectionary by Bayard Hale Jones (New York: Morehouse-Gorham Co., 1944). An introduction to the schedule of Psalms and lessons of the Daily Offices, showing their thematic relations to the seasons of the Church Year and to the Holy Communion.

THE PSALMS (see *The Holy Scriptures,* p. 202):

The Religion of the Psalms by J. M. Powis Smith (Chicago: University of Chicago Press, 1922).

The Praises of Israel, Studies Literary and Religious in the Psalms by John Paterson (New York: Scribners, 1950).

The Psalms and Their Meaning for Today by Samuel Terrien (Indianapolis: Bobbs-Merrill Co., Inc., 1952).
These three books, designed for the general reader, present the religious teachings of the Psalms and their enduring relevance for faith and worship today.

THE LITANY:

An Exposition of the Litany by A. C. A. Hall (Milwaukee: The Young Churchman Co., 1914).
Reflections on the Litany by Charles Gore (London: Mowbray, 1932).
Devotional commentaries on the prayers of the Litany, full of solid theological content.
The People's Prayers, Being Some Considerations on the Use of the Litany in Public Worship by E. G. Cuthbert Atchley (Alcuin Club Tracts, VI; London: Longmans, Green and Co., 1906). A brief survey of the history of the use of the Litany.

CHAPTER SEVEN:
THE HOLY COMMUNION

Anglican Liturgies edited by J. H. Arnold for the Alcuin Club (New York: Oxford University Press, 1939). An edition of the service in the various Prayer Books of the Anglican Communion.
The Liturgy of the Church of England before and after the Reformation together with the Service of Holy Communion of the Episcopal Church in the United States edited with an Introduction and Notes by Stephen A. Hurlbut (Washington: St. Albans Press, 1941). A handsome edition of the rite, giving in parallel columns the Sarum use, and the 1549 and 1928 rites.
Handbook to the Christian Liturgy by James Norman (London: S.P.C.K., 1944). A comparison of the Eucharistic litur-

gies of all the Churches, East and West, showing what they have in common and what is distinctive to each.

HISTORICAL:

The Early Eucharist by Felix L. Cirlot (London: S.P.C.K., 1939). A scholarly study of the origins of the Holy Communion and its development in the first two centuries. Contains a lengthy bibliography of the subject. For the advanced student.

The Anaphora or Great Eucharistic Prayer by Walter Howard Frere (London: S.P.C.K., 1938). A scholarly study of the development of the Consecration Prayer.

The Holy Communion by Darwell Stone (London: Longmans, Green and Co., 1904). Special emphasis on the history of doctrine.

The Eucharistic Office of the Book of Common Prayer by Leslie Wright (London: S.P.C.K., 1919). A brief, general account of the historical background of the English rite, both in ritual and ceremonial.

Eucharistic Faith and Practice, Evangelical and Catholic by Yngve Brilioth (London: S.P.C.K., 1930). A masterful treatment of the meaning of the Holy Communion in the early, medieval, and modern Church, Catholic, Anglican, Lutheran and Reformed.

The Lord's Supper and the Liturgy by Walter Lowrie (New York: Longmans, Green and Co., 1943). A brief interpretation of the Last Supper, with a commentary, historical and practical, upon the American rite of Holy Communion.

The Scottish Communion Office, 1764, by John Dowden (New edition; Oxford: Clarendon Press, 1922). A definitive study of the Scottish service that was brought to the American Church by Bishop Seabury.

Bishop Seabury's Communion-Office Reprinted in Facsimile

230 ·

with an Historical Sketch and Notes by Samuel Hart (New York: T. Whittaker, 1883).

INTERPRETATION:

The Sacrament of the Altar by W. C. E. Newbolt (London: Longmans, Green and Co., 1908).

Personality and Holy Communion, A Fresh Approach to the Eucharist by D. S. Guy (London: Mowbray, 1931).

The Church's Offering, A Brief Study of Eucharistic Worship by Henry de Candole (London: Mowbray, 1935).

The English Liturgy in the Light of the Bible by W. K. Lowther Clarke (London: S.P.C.K., 1940).

Strange Victory, A Study of the Holy Communion by Max Warren (London: Canterbury Press, 1946).

A Lively Sacrifice by Harold Sly (London: Mowbray, 1947).

The Holy Communion, A Symposium, edited by Hugh Martin (London: SCM Press, 1947). Interpretations of leaders of various denominations.

The Christian Sacrifice, A Study of the Eucharist in the Life of the Christian Church by W. Norman Pittenger (New York: Oxford University Press, 1951).

A Little Anthology of the Holy Eucharist compiled by Olive M. Hardy (London: S.P.C.K., 1924). Devotional materials from all ages on the meaning of Holy Communion.

The Mystery of Sacrifice, A Meditation on the Liturgy by Evelyn Underhill (London: Longmans, Green and Co., 1938).

PRACTICAL:

The Parish Communion, A Book of Essays edited by A. G. Hebert (London: S.P.C.K., 1937). Historical, theological, and practical discussions of the Holy Communion as the principal corporate worship of the Church.

Sunday Morning: The New Way, Papers on the Parish Communion edited by Brother Edward (London: S.P.C.K., 1938). Practical discussions of the celebration of the Eucharist in parishes at the principal service on Sundays.

CHAPTER EIGHT:
CHRISTIAN INITIATION: BAPTISM, INSTRUCTION AND CONFIRMATION

The Origin and Significance of the New Testament Baptism by H. G. Marsh (Manchester: Manchester University Press, 1941).

The New Testament Doctrine of Baptism by W. F. Flemington (London: S.P.C.K., 1948).

Baptism in the New Testament by Oscar Cullmann, translated by J. K. S. Reid (London: SCM Press, Ltd., 1950). Three outstanding and scholarly studies of the New Testament practice of Baptism and its historical background. The latter two books also contain a defense of infant Baptism.

The Offices of Baptism and Confirmation by T. Thompson (Cambridge: Cambridge University Press, 1914). A technical handbook tracing the development of the initiation rites of the Eastern and Western Churches.

Baptism and Christian Archaeology by Clement F. Rogers (Oxford: Clarendon Press, 1903). A scholarly investigation of the mode of Baptism from ancient, archaeological sources.

Holy Baptism by Darwell Stone (London: Longmans, Green and Co., 1899). A standard treatment of the subject.

Confirmation by A. C. A. Hall (London: Longmans, Green and Co., 1900). A companion volume to the foregoing work.

Confirmation or the Laying on of Hands by various writers, 2 volumes (London: S.P.C.K., 1926-27). The first volume contains essays on the history and doctrine of Confirmation; the second volume deals with practical problems of its administration.

"Bishoping" by Oscar Hardman (London: S.P.C.K., n.d.). A masterly little book on the meaning of Confirmation.

Confirmation in the Modern World by Matthias Laros, translated by George Sayer (New York: Sheed and Ward, 1938). A valuable study of the subject from a Roman Catholic viewpoint.

The Theology of Confirmation in Relation to Baptism by Gregory Dix (Westminster: Dacre Press, 1946). In this lecture Dom Dix argues that Confirmation is necessary to Christian initiation, since in Baptism the Holy Spirit is not conferred.

Christian Initiation by A. E. J. Rawlinson (London: S.P.C.K., 1947). A defense of the Prayer Book pattern of initiation on the basis of New Testament evidence.

The Seal of the Spirit by G. W. H. Lampe (London: Longmans, Green and Co., 1951). "A Study in the Doctrine of Baptism and Confirmation in the New Testament and the Fathers." A most important work of careful scholarship, maintaining that Baptism is full initiation, with the gift of the Spirit, whereas Confirmation is a valuable but distinct and additional gift of the Spirit. Contains an excellent bibliography.

Confirmation Today. Being the Schedule attached to the Interim Reports of the Joint Committees on Baptism, Confirmation, and Holy Communion, as presented to the Convocations of Canterbury and York in October, 1944 (London: Press and Publications Board, 1944).

Baptism Today. Being the Schedule attached to the Second Interim Reports of the Joint Committees on Baptism, Confirmation, and Holy Communion, as presented to the Convocations of Canterbury and York in October, 1949 (London: Press and Publications Board, 1949).

The Theology of Christian Initiation. Being the Report of a Theological Commission appointed by the Archbishops of

Canterbury and York to advise on the Relations between Baptism, Confirmation and Holy Communion (London: S.P.C.K., 1949). These three reports are the basis of current discussions in Anglicanism on the relation of Baptism and Confirmation.

Prayer Book Studies: I. Baptism and Confirmation (New York: The Church Pension Fund, 1950). A report of the Standing Liturgical Commission of the Episcopal Church, containing a suggested revision of the rites of Baptism and Confirmation, with an introductory and explanatory essay.

CREEDS:

The Earliest Christian Confessions by Oscar Cullmann, translated by J. K. S. Reid (London: Lutterworth Press, 1949).

Early Christian Baptism and the Creed, A Study in Ante-Nicene Theology (The Bellarmine Series, XIII) by Joseph Crehan (London: Burns Oates and Washbourne, Ltd., 1950).

Early Christian Creeds by J. N. D. Kelly (New York: Longmans, Green and Co., 1950).

Three scholarly and technical works treating the origin of the Creeds. Their relation to the baptismal rites is thoroughly presented.

CHAPTER NINE:
"OTHER RITES AND CEREMONIES"

HOLY MATRIMONY:

The Bond of Honour, A Marriage Handbook by Burton Scott Easton and Howard Chandler Robbins (New York: Macmillan, 1938).

The Marriage Service and After by Hervey C. Parke (Milwaukee: Morehouse Publishing Co., 1928).

Two brief, but excellent manuals of instruction in the

meaning of Christian marriage, based on the Prayer Book service.

VISITATION OF THE SICK:

Healing: Pagan and Christian by George Gordon Dawson (London: S.P.C.K., 1935). A comprehensive history of rites and methods of healing used in the Church, and in pre-Christian times.

Body and Soul by Percy Dearmer (New York: E. P. Dutton and Co., 1909). An Enquiry into the Effect of Religion upon Health, with a Description of Christian Works of Healing from the New Testament to the Present Day. Also discusses the Prayer Book rites.

The Anointing of the Sick in Scripture and Tradition by F. W. Puller (London: S.P.C.K., 1910). A standard history of Unction.

Exorcism and the Healing of the Sick by Reginald Maxwell Woolley (London: S.P.C.K., 1932). A study of healing in the early Church.

Stretching Forth Thine Hand to Heal by R. A. Richard Spread (New York: Morehouse Publishing Co., 1937). A description of modern methods of religious healing, with use of unction and laying on of hands.

Prayer Book Studies: III. *The Order for the Ministration of the Sick* (New York: The Church Pension Fund, 1951). Prepared by the Standing Liturgical Commission of the Episcopal Church, a suggested revision of the Prayer Book rites, with an introduction on the history of the Visitation Office.

The Church and the Ministry of Healing, Essays by Bishop Hough and Others, edited by T. W. Crafer (London: S.P.C.K., 1934). A presentation of present practice in the Church of England.

Death and Burial in Christian Antiquity by Alfred C. Rush (Washington: Catholic University of America Press, 1941). A scholarly study of the concept of death, and rites connected with death and burial in early Christian times.

CHAPTER TEN:
THE MINISTRY OF THE CHURCH

Essays on the Early History of the Church and the Ministry by Various Writers, edited by H. B. Swete (2nd edition; London: Macmillan, 1921). Historical studies of the origins of the threefold ministry, apostolic succession, and early forms of ordination.

The Church and Its Organization in Primitive and Catholic Times by Walter Lowrie (London: Longmans, Green and Co., 1904). Valuable as a study of the origins of the ministry in relation to its liturgical functions.

The Roman Pontifical, A History and Commentary by Pierre Puniet (New York: Longmans, Green and Co., 1932). A brief survey of the development of rites of ordination in the Latin Church.

The Question of Anglican Orders, Letters to a Layman by Dom Gregory Dix (Westminster: Dacre Press, 1944). A defense of the Prayer Book Ordinal in simple terms for the laity.

Holy Orders by A. R. Whitham (London: Longmans, Green and Co., 1903). A historical, doctrinal and practical study.

Ministerial Priesthood by R. C. Moberly (London: John Murray, 1919). A classic work on the meaning of priesthood, with a rationale of the ministerial orders of the Church. For advanced readers.

Sacrificial Priesthood, Historical Origins and Developments by Joseph Barker (Westminster: Dacre Press, 1941). A brief booklet for the laity, explaining the meaning of Christian priesthood, with some account of its origin and function.

Index

James, Epistle of, 192, 194.
Jerusalem, Church of, 78, 108.
John the Baptist, St., 49, 118, 168.
Jubilate, 131.
Judaism, 35, 68, 69-71, 102, 105-106, 160, 168, 172, 175, 190.
Justin Martyr, St., 73-75, 192.

Kiss of Peace, 76.
Kyrie eleison, 26, 35, 151-152.

Last Supper, 71, 73, 142-147, 160, 199.
Laying on of Hands, *see* Confirmation, Ordination, Unction.
Lectionary, *see* Lessons.
Lent, 105, 109-110, 119, 130, 180.
Lessons, 36-38, 74, 97, 128, 129-131, 152-154; *see* Bible, Epistle, Gospel.
Litany, 61, 80, 97, 99, 123, 133, 136-138, 149, 151, 203; of Ordinations, 203.
Liturgy, 46-51, 61-66, 67-68, 77-81, 85, 198.
Lord's Prayer, 41, 66, 73, 126, 136, 138, 141, 159, 162, 181, 182, 183, 184, 188.
Lord's Supper, *see* Holy Communion.
Luther, Martin, 54, 88, 137, 178.
Lutherans, 68.

Magnificat, 131.
Martyrs, 3-6, 8, 11, 29, 74, 77, 165, 169.
Mary, St., 77, 102, 118, 190.
Mass, 52, 54, 84, 141, 151-152, 195.
Matrimony, 14, 47, 58-59, 85, 98, 102, 148, 187-190.
Medieval worship, 54, 68, 82-86, 137, 148, 156, 178-179, 189, 192, 201-202.
Memorial, in Holy Communion, 104, 159, 161.
Merbecke, John, 54.
Methodists, 68.
Ministry, Orders of, 50, 173-174, 183, 198-205; of laity, 205-208.
Missal, 81.

Monasticism, 49, 53-54, 80-82, 135, 140.
Morning Prayer, 25, 26, 36, 56, 60, 81, 88, 103, 108, 123-136, 138-140, 149.
Mozarabic rite, 80.
Music, 48, 53-55, 81, 161, 189-190.

Name of God, in Baptism, 62, 171-172, 182; of Christ, 45, 172.
Nestorians, 78.
New Testament, *see* Bible.
Nicaea, Council of, 109; *see* Creed.
Nunc Dimittis, 131.

Oblation, *see* Offering, Offertory, Sacrifice.
Offering, 43-45, 139, 155, 156-158, 160, 163.
Offertory, in Holy Communion, 44, 60, 76, 89, 154-159, 203.
Old Testament, *see* Bible.
Order, in worship, 51-52, 74.
Ordinal, 201-205.
Ordination, 200-205.
Orthodox Churches, *see* Eastern Orthodox Churches.
Oxford Movement, 149.

Palm Sunday, 108.
Passover, 69, 105-106, 107, 116, 130, 142.
Paul, St., 32, 49, 52, 101, 107, 115, 141, 164, 173, 175, 199, 206.
Penitence, 19, 30-35, 51-52, 99, 103, 110, 124-126, 137, 138, 155, 158-159, 191.
Penitential Office, 97.
Pentecost, 69, 105, 107, 108, 121, 169; *see* Whitsunday.
Persecution, 3-5, 8-11, 77, 108, 109, 115, 137, 180.
Peter, St., 115; Epistle of, 206-207.
Petition, 17, 28, 40-44, 132, 138.
Pie, 85.
Plainsong, 54, 79.
Praise, 17, 19, 23, 26-30, 36, 51-52, 124, 126, 129, 131, 137, 160.
Prayer, 27-28, 40-45, 132-134; for

the departed, 84, 113-114, 158, 196.

Prayer Book, history of, 35-36, 47, 87-94, 147.

Preaching, see Sermon.

Pre-Lent, 110, 130.

Presbyter, 73, 200-205.

Presbyterians, 68.

Presentation, feast of, 118.

Priest, see Presbyter.

Processions, 57, 60, 61, 108, 138, 153, 195.

Psalms, 19, 21, 22, 28, 53, 55, 70, 74, 81, 97, 107, 126-129, 131, 132, 136, 151, 191, 193, 194, 195-196.

Purgatory, 84, 89.

Purification of St. Mary, 118.

Puritans, 46-47, 63, 67, 91.

Quakers, 52.

Quiñones, Cardinal, 87.

Rationale, 52, 130; see Order.

Real Presence, 89, 90, 144.

Reformation, 47, 54, 59, 68, 85, 86-90, 135, 141, 148-149, 178.

Regeneration, 170, 176.

Requiem, 114, 195.

Revelation, 25, 35-40, 101, 129-130; see Word.

Ritual, 17, 51, 52-56, 60-61, 77.

Rogation Days, 80.

Roman Catholic Church, 47, 52, 60, 68, 79-81, 85, 86, 114, 115, 118, 137, 173, 174, 177.

Russia, 78.

Sabbath, see Sunday.

Sacraments, 39, 56, 61-62, 123, 138-139, 178, 183.

Sacrifice, 7, 34, 44, 59, 69-70, 144-145, 161, 163, 165, 207-208.

Saint's Days, 77, 84, 88, 113-115.

Salutation, 151, 153.

Sanctus, 27, 29, 35, 55, 159, 160.

Sarum, Use of, 85.

Scottish Prayer Book, 92-93, 160.

Scriptures, see Bible.

Seabury, Bishop Samuel, 92.

Septuagesima, 130; see Pre-Lent.

Septuagint, 48, 185.

Sermon, 39-40, 53, 56, 139, 149, 151, 154, 203.

Sick, Visitation of the, 98, 191-195.

Sin, 31-34, 99, 125, 158, 191, 192.

Sponsors, 180, 181.

Sunday, 8, 19-21, 38, 98, 107, 111-113, 122, 139, 147-150, 179, 201.

Symbols, 24, 48, 56-58, 61.

Synagogue, 35, 69-71, 72, 112.

Syria, liturgy in, 78.

Table, holy, 57-59, 73, 153, 155, 156.

Te Deum, 27, 131, 136.

Temple, 48, 53, 69-70.

Tertullian, 5.

Thanksgiving, Day, 126; General, 136; see Praise.

Thomas Becket, St., 121.

Toleration, 5, 8-12.

Transubstantiation, 89.

Trinity, Season, 121-122; Sunday, 121.

Unction, 192-194.

Veni, Creator Spiritus, 202, 204.

Venite, 25, 126, 136.

Versicles and Responses, 55, 126, 132.

Vestments, 57, 60.

Visitation of the Sick, 98, 191-195.

Weddings, see Matrimony.

Wesley, John, 149.

Whitsunday, 105, 110, 120-122; see Pentecost.

Word, of God, 36, 39-40, 52-54, 57, 124, 129-132, 150, 154, 188; see Bible.

Worship, judgment in, 25-26, 34, 52, 99, 124, 125, 157-158; social values in, 12-13, 15-16, 18, 21-22.

Year, Christian, 38, 56, 60, 97-122, 130, 133.

Zwingli, 148.

12-1152-C-25-20